EUROPE IN TRANSITION

GARLAND REFERENCE LIBRARY
OF THE HUMANITIES
(VOL. 875)

EUROPE IN TRANSITION
A Select, Annotated Bibliography of the Twelfth-Century Renaissance

Chris D. Ferguson

GARLAND PUBLISHING, INC. • NEW YORK & LONDON
1989

© 1989 Chris D. Ferguson
All rights reserved

Library of Congress Cataloging-in-Publication Data

Ferguson, Chris D., 1951–
  Europe in transition.

  (Garland reference library of the humanities ;
vol. 875)
  Includes index.
  1. Europe—History—476-1492—Bibliography.
  2. Twelfth century—Bibliography. I. Title. II. Series.
  Z2000.F45 1989 [D201.8] 016.9401'82   88-31033
  ISBN 0–8240–3722–7 (alk. paper)

Printed on acid-free, 250-year-life paper
Manufactured in the United States of America

CONTENTS

Acknowledgments vii
Preface ix

1.0 General

1.1 General Studies on the Twelfth Century (1-41) 1

2.0 Society

2.1. The Structure of Society
    2.1.1 General (42-104) 11
    2.1.2 Special Groups (105-134) 19
2.2 Social Customs and Conditions (135-166) 25
2.3 Social and Religious Movements (167-211) 31

3.0 Politics, Government, and Armed Conflict

3.1 National Monarchies and the Church (212-321) 39
3.2 Local and Regional Studies (322-363) 53
3.3 Law, Administration, Taxation, and Institutions (364-414) . 59
3.4 Armed Conflict (415-455) 67

4.0 Culture

4.1 Religious Life and Spirituality (456-481) 73
4.2 Monasticism and Monastic Culture (482-538). 77
4.3 Learning and Intellectual Life
    4.3.1 General (539-575) 85
    4.3.2 Theology and Philosophy (576-608) 90
    4.3.3 Biblical Studies and Exegesis (609-620) 96
    4.3.4 Science and Natural Philosophy (621-638) 98
    4.3.5 The Universities and Schools (639-657) 101

4.4 Language and Literature
   4.4.1 General (658-671) 104
   4.4.2 Latin (672-717) 107
   4.4.3 Vernacular (718-772) 114
4.5 Art and Architecture (773-820) 122
4.6 Performing Arts (821-841) 129

5.0 Economic Life and the Physical Environment

5.1 The Economy, Urbanization, and Population (842-865) 133
5.2 Agrarian Studies and Estate Administration (866-899) . . . 136

Person-as-Subject Index 143
Author Index 147

ACKNOWLEDGMENTS

The author of a bibliography several years in the making necessarily owes debts of gratitude to many people. First among those to whom I am indebted is Calvin Boyer, University Librarian for the University of California, Irvine. While serving as Social Sciences Bibliographer at UCI, I benefited greatly from his commitment to the professional development of librarians, including provision of microcomputing and word processing equipment, travel opportunities, and generous research grants that underwrote most of the expenses of this project. The intellectual (not to mention moral) support of Pat Ferguson, particularly her knowledge of computer programming and technology, has been of great value. Without her assistance in these and other ways, completion of this bibliography would have been considerably more tedious. I am grateful to Ted Sheldon, Director of the University of Missouri-Kansas City Libraries, fellow medievalist, and ALA comrade-in-arms, for contributing the annotations in section 5.0 as well as extensive editorial acumen.

PREFACE

Europe in Transition: A Select, Annotated Bibliography of the Twelfth-Century Renaissance consists of annotated citations to selected studies that examine the major social, political, cultural, and economic currents of a critical period in the development of Western civilization. The purpose of this bibliography is to assist intellectual and bibliographic access to the twelfth-century renaissance by bringing together and commenting on the leading scholarly works on the period. While orientation to a particular century is to some extent unfashionable as historical studies increasingly de-emphasize periodization, chronological demarcation of the twelfth century remains quite useful to medievalists. Seminars, conferences, and much scholarship focus on this period as a conceptual unit.

In recent years historians have become increasingly parochial in their research interests, a trend that includes medievalists studying the twelfth century. At the same time historians have become more aware of the twelfth century as a period of great importance in medieval history--indeed, in Western history generally. Recognition of the importance of this period became widespread with the 1927 publication of C.H. Haskins's The Renaissance of the Twelfth Century, a study that engendered several works prior to World War II. Twelfth-century studies received a later boost with Colin Morris's 1972 book, The Discovery of the Individual, 1050-1200. In the last decade a great number of books and articles that focus on the twelfth century as a unique period in medieval civilization have appeared.

The body of research on the twelfth-century renaissance is now so extensive that scholars who wish to identify the literature of a topic face formidable barriers in cumbersome bibliographic sources. International Medieval Bibliography, the field's principal current literature index, does not allow chronological access to its contents except by visually scanning each item within a broad subject category. The recent six-volume supplement to L.J. Paetow's 1931 bibliography of medieval history, Literature of Medieval History, 1930-1975 (1981; compiled and edited by Gray C. Boyce), is a milestone in the bibliography of medieval history. Unfortunately for students of the twelfth century, the work is arranged by topical, chronological, and geographical categories too broad for the convenient isolation of works related to the period, contains only a name index, and is not as comprehensive as one might expect. E.U. Crosby, C.J. Bishko, and R.L. Kellogg's Medieval Studies: A Bibliographical Guide (1983) also fails to isolate easily works specific to the twelfth century.

Increasing specialization within twelfth-century studies and greater awareness of the importance of this scholarship warrant a bibliography devoted to the twelfth-century renaissance. Europe in Transition: A Select, Annotated Bibliography of the Twelfth-Century Renaissance fills a gap in the bibliography of the literature of medieval history by facilitating access to twelfth-century scholarship. Entries in the bibliography are drawn from all materials published before, and books and leading journals published during, 1987.

How to Use This Bibliography

This bibliography puts both novices and advanced users in touch with leading works on particular aspects of the twelfth-century renaissance, thus providing both intellectual and bibliographic points of departure for research on the period. With convenient access to the important works in an area of study, the student or scholar can proceed to construct a larger, more personalized bibliography by allowing items in this bibliography to provide pathways to other works, especially through citation searching.

Citation searching combines the advantages of a select bibliography and a comprehensive journal index by employing items from the former to locate relevant items in the latter. <u>Arts & Humanities Citation Index</u> and <u>Social Sciences Citation Index</u>, available in nearly all academic and large public libraries, index both articles and footnotes in articles from thousands of journals in their respective disciplines. One can select a seminal book or article (such as Morris's <u>Discovery of the Individual</u>), then determine who in the years since its publication has cited the work in journal articles.

Because useful articles on a given subject are likely to cite the leading works on that subject, citation searching provides the researcher with relatively convenient access to the current literature of a subject once some important works have been identified. Citation searching thereby circumvents many of the inherent problems of subject classification and keyword indexing used in various bibliographies, indexes, and library catalogs that frustrate even strong-willed bibliophiles. Examination of these <u>citing</u> articles will in turn lead to books and other material related to the subject at hand that have escaped discovery through either systematic or serendipitous bibliographic efforts.

Citation searching in <u>Social Sciences Citation Index</u> and <u>Arts & Humanities Citation Index</u> may also be accomplished in a computer-assisted fashion through online retrieval services in most academic and large public libraries. Whether done manually or with the assistance of a computer, citation searching in either index has certain limitations and should be regarded as only one step in the bibliographic component in research.

While <u>Europe in Transition: A Select, Annotated Bibliography of the Twelfth-Century Renaissance</u> provides a starting point for ventures into the history of twelfth-century Europe, this bibliography, even when used with citation searching, should not be regarded as the sole bibliographic source for twelfth-century history. The reader is advised to consult the list of bibliographic sources below for more specialized and narrowly-focused resources. Especially useful as a point of departure is <u>Dictionary of the Middle Ages</u>, an encyclopedia with extensive articles and bibliographies.

Selection Criteria

Annotated entries for <u>Europe in Transition: A Select, Annotated Bibliography of the Twelfth-Century Renaissance</u> were chosen on the basis of 1) their scholarly value within the literature and 2) the extent to which they provide bibliographic access to related literature by means of either notes or bibliographies. Of these criteria, scholarly value is the weightier consideration. Analytical works that confront the ideas of change or renaissance in the twelfth century are preferred, though many descriptive works are included in areas lacking an adequate number of studies that interpret the topic in the context of larger twelfth-century currents. The economic history of the period is discussed less easily independent of larger chronological spans than other topics relevant to the twelfth century. Thus, items in section 5.0 tend to cover larger chronological periods than works in the preceding sections.

Works of lesser scholarly value with exceptional bibliographic merit are included in some categories, but not to the exclusion of works of scholarly importance. Annotations indicate the reason for selection when considerations other than scholarship pertain. Unannotated citations listed at the end of each subsection were selected using a less rigid application of the above criteria, with recency of publication and importance of author providing guidance.

Only secondary works are cited, including books, articles, dissertations, and bibliographies. General texts or surveys are excluded except when oriented to a relatively narrow area or topic (e.g., art or music) and when an extended discussion of twelfth-century aspects of the subject appear. Special emphasis is placed on post-World War II publications but outstanding earlier works are included. No strict geographic limitations are maintained, but there is a predominance of works in English, German, and French. Some items in Spanish and Italian are included. Beginning students will not find introductory textbooks, works on methodology, source collections, or source criticism <u>per se</u> in this bibliography; these readers should consult a basic handbook or guide to the study of medieval history.

Bibliographic Sources

The following bibliographic sources supplemented the author's knowledge of the literature and references obtained from books, articles, and catalogs. Items bearing asterisks were searched in their computer-based versions.

Current indexes and bibliographies (as available through June 1987): International Medieval Bibliography, Recently Published Articles, Writings on British History, Arts & Humanities Citation Index, *Social Sciences Citation Index, *MLA Bibliography, *Comprehensive Dissertation Index (which includes Dissertation Abstracts International), Music Index, Art Index, *Philosopher's Index, and *Religion Index.

Retrospective bibliographies (not including bibliographies cited in this volume): Gray C. Boyce, Literature of Medieval History, 1930-1975, 6 vols. (Millwood, NY: Kraus International, 1981) and E.U. Crosby, C.J. Bishko, and R.L. Kellogg, Medieval Studies: A Bibliographical Guide (New York: Garland, 1983).

Continuing bibliographies in journals: Isis: An International Review Devoted to the History of Science and its Cultural Influences and Revue d'histoire ecclésiastique.

The current indexes Internationale Bibliographie der Zeitschriftenliteratur and L'année philologique, and the continuing bibliography in Cahiers de civilisation médiévale, do not accommodate subject searches of the nature required for this bibliography.

Europe in Transition

1.0 GENERAL

1.1 General Studies on the Twelfth Century

1. Benson, Robert L. and G. Constable, eds., Renaissance and Renewal in the Twelfth Century (Cambridge, MA: Harvard University Press, 1982).
   A collection of interpretive articles by internationally respected medievalists presented at a 1977 conference. Essays cover the topics of religion, education, society and the individual; law, politics, and history; philosophy and science, literature, and the arts. Contributions include bibliographic notes, including G. Ladner's opening survey of twelfth-century conceptions of renewal.

2. Benton, John F., "Consciousness of Self and Perceptions of Individuality," in R. Benson and G. Constable, eds., Renaissance and Renewal in the Twelfth Century (Cambridge, MA: Harvard University Press, 1981), 263-95.
   Considers conventional explanations for changes in perceptions of individuality before settling on a combination of the Germanic political tradition of "individualism," changing economic conditions, intellectual diversification, and the shift from a guilt- to a shame-oriented culture.

3. ------, "Individualism and Conformity in Medieval Western Europe," in A. Banani and S. Vryonis, Jr., eds., Individualism and

Conformity in Classical Islam (Wiesbaden: Harrassowitz, 1977), 145-58.
> Begins with a survey of the definitions and historical uses of the term "individualism," then speaks broadly on manifestations of individualism in the Middle Ages.

4. Brown, Peter, "Society and the Supernatural: A Medieval Change," Daedalus, 104:2(Spring 1975), 133-51.
> Focuses on changing attitudes toward the ordeal and the supernatural to support the argument that a disengagement of the sacred from the profane occurred at this time.

5. Bynum, Caroline Walker, "Did the Twelfth Century Discover the Individual?" Journal of Ecclesiastical History, 31(1980), 1-17.
> Examines religious life and writing to resolve the apparent paradox between "the discovery of the individual" and a greater awareness of groups and group roles. Greater self-awareness about having and making social choices, in relation to individuals and to groups, is held responsible for both phenomena. Reprinted in her Jesus as Mother: Studies in the Spirituality of the High Middle Ages (Berkeley: University of California Press, 1984). See related item 464 in section 4.1, a response to this article.

6. Cantor, Norman F., "Creativity and Rebellion," The Meaning of the Middle Ages (Boston: Allyn and Bacon, 1973), 203-48.
> Centers on a liberation movement as the common denominator in the creative outburst of the twelfth century, a movement that was socialized and otherwise controlled by traditional leadership in the thirteenth century.

7. Clagett, Marshall et al., eds., Twelfth-Century Europe and the Foundations of Modern Society (Madison: University of Wisconsin Press, 1961).
> Proceedings of a 1957 symposium. Participants include R. Klibansky, U. Holmes, J. Strayer, E. Kantorowicz, and G. von Grunebaum. Nine contributions are grouped as "Thought in European Society," "Transitions in Economy and Society," and "Eastern Influences on European Culture."

8. Duby, Georges, "The Culture of the Knightly Class: Audience and Patronage," in R. Benson and G. Constable, eds., Renaissance and Renewal in the Twelfth Century (Cambridge, MA: Harvard University Press, 1982), 248-62.
   Under the rubrics of "Growth and Its Effects," "Patronage," and "Audience," Duby suggests ways in which socioeconomic structures relate to cultural phenomena.

9. Ferguson, Wallace K., "The Revolt of the Medievalists: The Renaissance Interpreted as Continuation of the Middle Ages," The Renaissance in Historical Thought (Boston: Houghton Mifflin, 1948), 329-85.
   Traces two historiographical developments in medieval studies: increased awareness of (and respect for) medieval culture, and diminished regard for what previously were seen as unique developments of the Renaissance. These approaches constitute a "revolt" led chiefly by American scholars that advances the notion of the Renaissance as a continuation of the Middle Ages.

10. Ferruolo, Stephen C., "The Twelfth-Century Renaissance," in W. Treadgold, ed., Renaissances Before the Renaissance: Cultural Revivals of Late Antiquity and the Middle Ages (Stanford: Stanford University Press, 1984), 114-43.
    Surveys the historiography of the twelfth-century renaissance, then assesses three different approaches to the problem: the aggregate, or all-inclusive approach; an approach that emphasizes humanism, including individuality; and an approach that focuses on changes in mentality. Extensive notes and short bibliography.

11. Gandillac, Maurice de and E. Jeauneau, eds., Entretiens sur la renaissance du 12e siècle: Cerisy-la-Salle, 21 au 30 juillet 1965 (Paris: Mouton, 1968).
    Contains contributions by several leading medievalists, including J. Chatillon on the school of St. Victor, R. Foreville on English political conscience, B. Smalley on biblical exegesis, J. Leclercq on the literary humanism of Bernard of Clairvaux, and R. Javelet on spiritual and courtly love.

12. Gwynn, Aubrey O., The Twelfth Century Reform (Dublin: C. Gill, 1968).
   So little has been written on Ireland in the twelfth century that this 68-page work, while not extraordinary, is important. The work discusses ecclesiastical reform, though it also includes brief discussions of St. Malachy and church-building, art, and architecture. Also see W.L. Warren, "The Interpretation of Twelfth-Century Irish History," Historical Studies: Papers Read Before the Irish Conference of Historians, 7(1969), 1-19.

13. Haskins, Charles H., The Renaissance of the Twelfth Century (Cambridge, MA: Harvard University Press, 1927).
   Nearly sixty years ago Haskins produced the first substantial work to recognize the importance of the twelfth century. The survey, which focuses on the Latin literature of the period, remains a useful general introduction.

14. Heer, Friedrich, Aufgang Europas: eine Studie zu den Zusammenhängen zwischen politischer Religiosität, Frömmigkeitsstil und dem Werden Europas im 12. Jahrhundert (Vienna: Europa, 1949).
   An early milestone in the historiography of twelfth-century studies. Heer explores the religiosity of the century in an effort to understand a period rife with conflict, controversy, and paradox.

15. ------, Mittelalter (Zurich: Kindler, 1961). Translated by J. Sondheimer as The Medieval World: Europe, 1100-1350 (New York: The New American Library, 1962).
   Begins with the twelfth century, then tells how the story turns out: The twelfth century was an "open society" followed by the "closed society" of succeeding centuries.

16. Holmes, Urban T., "The Idea of a Twelfth-Century Renaissance," Speculum, 26(1951), 643-51.
   Focuses on twelfth-century vernacular literature with reference to the concepts of renaissance and humanism broadly defined (cf. conservative uses of these terms by W. Nitze, E. Panofsky, and E. Sanford in this section). The result is a high regard for the literary creativity of the period and a

strong argument for associating the term "renaissance" with the twelfth century.

17. Knowles, David, "The Humanism of the Twelfth Century," The Historian and Character and Other Essays (Cambridge, England: Cambridge University Press, 1963), 16-30.
>   Encapsulates the essence of a "sympathetic humanism" that characterizes the period 1050-1150. The flowering of a literary culture, neo-classicism, and increased awareness of the individual all contributed to a new humanism that soon lost its momentum but left an enduring legacy. See related item 28.

18. McGinn, Bernard J., "Renaissance, Humanism, and the Interpretation of the Twelfth Century," Journal of Religion, 55(1975), 444-55.
>   Surveys the principal historiographical schools up to the mid-1970s. A good point of departure for one who wishes to acquire an overview of the leading general interpretations of the twelfth century.

19. Morris, Colin, The Discovery of the Individual, 1050-1200 (New York: Harper & Row, 1972).
>   Covering much ground in a relatively short tour de force, Morris describes new departures in conceptions of individuality that emerged in virtually every aspect of twelfth-century life.

20. Murray, Alexander, Reason and Society in the Middle Ages (Oxford: Oxford University Press, 1978).
>   A social history of reason, roughly 1100-1300, that investigates the influence of commerce on rationality, reason as a social force, and some of the sociological effects of the elevation of reason as a cultural ideal. Includes a substantial bibliography.

21. Nitze, William A., "The So-Called Twelfth Century Renaissance," Speculum, 23(1948), 464-71.
>   Classicism was revived only to a limited extent in the twelfth century rather than truly reborn as in the later

Italian Renaissance, and the former period should not bear the epithet "renaissance."

22. Packard, Sidney R., <u>12th Century Europe: An Interpretive Essay</u> (Amherst: University of Massachusetts Press, 1973).
   Provides a general introduction to the twelfth century with a textbook approach that balances the approaches of highly interpretive and narrowly focused works on the twelfth century. Factual material, prevailing scholarly views, and Packard's interpretations are interlaced throughout.

23. Panofsky, Erwin, ""Renaissance and Renascences," <u>Renaissance and Renascences in Western Art</u> (Stockholm: Almqvist & Wiksell, 1960), 42-113.
   Revision of "Renaissance or Renascences," <u>Kenyon Review</u>, 6(1944), 201-36. Explores the natures and interrelations of medieval "renascences" and the Italian "renaissance," standing firmly with those who regard the latter as <u>the</u> renaissance. Concludes that the Italian renaissance of classical literature and art was preceded by ninth- and twelfth-century renascences of different scale and structure.

24. Radding, Charles M., <u>A World Made by Men: Cognition and Society, 400-1200</u> (Chapel Hill: University of North Carolina Press, 1985).
   Draws heavily on the Piagetian cognitive theory of moral development. Precipitated by major changes in political and educational structures, the twelfth century experienced a major shift in cultural (particularly interpersonal) and intellectual values that account for the emergence of a cognitive structure appreciably different from that of the early Middle Ages. See also his "Evolution of Medieval Mentalities: A Cognitive-Structural Approach," <u>American Historical Review</u>, 83(1978), 577-97.

25. Sanford, Eva Matthews, "The Twelfth Century--Renaissance or Proto-Renaissance?" <u>Speculum</u>, 26(1951), 635-42.
   Surveys the achievements of the twelfth century and considers the implications of regarding the period as either a renaissance or proto-renaissance (cf. E. Panofsky, above). Concludes both terms are inadequate and recommends we "be

satisfied to let the twelfth century stand on its own merits as a dynamic period of mediaeval culture."

26. Smalley, Beryl, "Ecclesiastical Attitudes to Novelty, c. 1100-c. 1250," <u>Studies in Medieval Thought and Learning from Abelard to Wyclif</u> (London: Hambledon Press, 1981), 97-115.
    Modern western civilization tends to regard change favorably. Medieval society tended not to do so--until there occurred a perceptible shift in the attitudes of ecclesiastics during the central Middle Ages. First appeared in D. Baker, ed., <u>Church, Society & Politics</u> (Oxford: Blackwell, 1975), 113-31.

27. Southern, Richard W., <u>The Making of the Middle Ages</u> (New Haven: Yale University Press, 1953).
    A classic interpretation of the late tenth to the early thirteenth centuries that addresses the particular without losing sight of larger ideas. Change, rennovation, and creative energy are the recurrent themes.

28. ------, "Medieval Humanism," <u>Medieval Humanism and Other Essays</u> (Oxford: Blackwell, 1970), 29-60.
    Assesses the twelfth and thirteenth centuries as "one of the greatest ages of humanism in the history of Europe: perhaps the greatest of all" (p. 31). Further argues that this progressive humanism was not highly regarded in later centuries by a negative, elitist humanism. See related item 17.

29. ------, "The Place of England in the Twelfth-Century Renaissance," <u>Medieval Humanism and Other Essays</u> (Oxford: Blackwell, 1970), 158-80.
    Acknowledges the greater achievements of the continent (especially France) during the period while surveying important contributions of the English. Chief among these are history writing, popular religious literature, and scientific interest. First published in <u>History,</u> 45(1960), 201-16. See related item 31, a response to this article.

30. Stock, Brian, <u>The Implications of Literacy: Written Language and Models of Interpretations in the Eleventh and Twelfth Centuries</u> (Princeton: Princeton University Press, 1983).

A wide-ranging study on "the rebirth of literacy and its effects upon the cultural life of the eleventh and twelfth centuries" that assesses the dynamics and implications of cultural change for human thought, communication, and action. Includes a lengthy bibliography. See related items 549 in section 4.3.1, and 658 and 663 in section 4.4.1.

31. Thomson, Rodney M., "England and the 12th-Century Renaissance," Past and Present, 101(1983), 3-21.

Responds to R.W. Southern (item 29) with a higher regard for the cultural contributions of England at this time. Refines "the intellectual and cultural map of twelfth-century Europe" and emphasizes native English intellectual traditions, English patronage, and English-born and English-educated achievers.

32. Ullmann, Walter, The Individual and Society in the Middle Ages (Baltimore: Johns Hopkins University Press, 1966).

Considers the individual within the context of medieval political theory. Details a descending theme of government typical of the early Middle Ages, examines the contribution of feudalism toward a greater regard for individual rights, and hails the later ascent of the citizen in England and the United States.

33. Weimar, Peter, ed., Die Renaissance der Wissenschaften im 12. Jahrhundert (Zurich: Artemis Press, 1981).

An important collection of essays that has not received much attention from British or American scholars. Contributions include P. Classen on the twelfth century generally, J. Ehlers on the schools, A. Zimmermann on theology and science, G. Otte on law, M. Schramm on Roger Bacon's concept of natural law, K. Fischer on music, and W. Kluxen on the concept of science. Articles are in German and most are amply referenced.

1.1 Additional Works

34. Bligny, Bernard, "L'église et le siècle de l'an mil au début du XIIe siècle," Cahiers de civilisation médiévale, 27(1984), 5-33.

35. Brooke, Christopher N., *The Twelfth Century Renaissance*, History of European Civilization Library (London: Thames and Hudson, 1969).
36. Duggan, Anne, "The New Europeans," in L. Smith, ed., *The Making of Britain: The Middle Ages* (London: Macmillan Press, 1985), 23-40.
37. Genicot, Léopold, "L'occident du Xe au XIIe siècle," *Revue d'histoire ecclésiastique*, 78(1983), 397-429.
38. Hollister, C. Warren, ed., *The Twelfth-Century Renaissance*, Major Issues in History (New York: John Wiley & Sons, 1969).
39. Kazhdan, A.P. and A.W. Epstein, *Change in Byzantine Culture in the Eleventh and Twelfth Centuries* (Berkeley: University of California Press, 1985).
40. Ward, John O., "Gothic Architecture, Universities and the Decline of the Humanities in Twelfth Century Europe," in L. Frappell, ed., *Principalities, Powers, and Estates: Studies in Medieval and Early Modern Government and Society* (Adelaide: Adelaide University Union Press, 1979), 65-75.
41. Young, Charles R., ed., *The Twelfth-Century Renaissance*, European Problem Studies (New York, 1977).

2.0 SOCIETY

2.1 The Structure of Society

2.1.1 General

42. Arnold, Benjamin, German Knighthood, 1050-1300 (Oxford: Oxford University Press, 1985).
   A broad study of the origins, nature, and development of the German ministerialage. Emphasizes structure and nature over development and consequences. Extensive bibliography.

43. Beech, George T., A Rural Society in Medieval France: The Gâtine of Poitou in the Eleventh and Twelfth Centuries (Baltimore: Johns Hopkins University Press, 1964).
   Examines patterns of settlement and colonization, the development of seigneurial institutions, and the structure of classes within a small pays in western France.

44. Bloch, Marc, La société féodale (Paris: A. Michel, 1939). Translated by L.A. Manyon as Feudal Society, 2 vols. (Chicago: University of Chicago Press, 1961).
   Not limited to the twelfth century, but Bloch's model of society, particularly the structure and essential characteristics of feudal relations, is the point of

departure for medieval social history, especially studies on the twelfth century.

45. Brett, Martin, The English Church under Henry I (London: Oxford University Press, 1975).
Primarily an administrative history that describes the organization of the upper echelons within the institutional Church. Reveals the structure and nature of various jurisdictions, offices, councils, and administrations from papacy to parish clergy. Includes a valuable bibliography of both primary and secondary works.

46. Brown, Elizabeth A., "The Tyranny of a Construct: Feudalism and Historians of Medieval Europe," American Historical Review, 19(1974), 1063-88.
Questions the use and meaning of "feudalism" and "feudal society" in a review article that analyzes prevailing concepts as well as leading scholarship on the subject. Another important conceptual and bibliographic orientation can be obtained with J. Prawer and S.N. Eisenstadt, "Feudalism," International Encyclopedia of the Social Sciences, 18 vols. (New York: Macmillan, 1968), 5:393-403.

47. Constable, Giles, "The Structure of Medieval Society According to the dictatores of the Twelfth Century," in K. Pennington and R. Somerville, eds., Law, Church, and Society: Essays in Honor of Stephan Kuttner (Philadelphia: University of Pennsylvania Press, 1977), 253-67.
A bird's eye view of the structure of twelfth-century society drawn from artes dictandi, letter-writting manuals that differed markedly in their perceptions of group distinctions and hierarchy.

48. Crosby, Everett U., "The Organization of the English Episcopate under Henry I," Studies in Medieval and Renaissance History, 4(1967), 1-88.
Presents two related but loosely connected studies: "The King's Bishops" details the ecclesiastical and feudal relationships between the king and his episcopate, and "The Bishop as Diocesan" describes the more practical realities of administering a diocese.

49. Debord, André, La société laïque dans les pays de la Charente, X-XIIe siècles (Paris: J. Picard, 1984).
A detailed examination of the social and political structure of the Charente River basin on the coast of Acquitaine. Method, data, and bibliography compensate for the lack of substantive general conclusions.

50. Duby, Georges, Les trois ordres: ou, l'imaginaire du féodalisme (Paris: Gallimard, 1978). Translated by A. Goldhammer as The Three Orders: Feudal Society Imagined (Chicago: University of Chicago Press, 1980).
Explores the origin, use, and implications of the model of a trifunctional society (those who pray, work, and fight) in northern France beginning in the latter part of the eleventh century. The model clearly was no longer valid by the early thirteenth century, yet became an increasingly popular concept. See item 61 for a review of this and related works by G. Dumézil, J. Batany, J. Grisward, and J. Le Goff. For a review of this and two other works by Duby (including item 142), see R.I. Moore, "Duby's Eleventh Century," History, 69(February 1984), 36-49. Also see Elizabeth A. Brown, "George Duby and the Three Orders," Viator, 17(1986), 51-64.

51. Evergates, Theodore, Feudal Society in the Bailliage of Troyes under the Counts of Champagne, 1152-1284 (Baltimore: Johns Hopkins University Press, 1975).
Uses both quantitative and traditional methods to analyze the social organization of a bailliage in southern Champagne. Focuses on the obligations, entitlements, and issues of status that formed the relationship between peasantry and aristocracy. Includes a substantial bibliography.

52. Fossier, Robert, Enfance de l'Europe, Xe-XIIe siècles: aspects économiques et sociaux, 2 vols. (Paris: Presses universitaires de France, 1982).
Presents a general framework for the central Middle Ages in the tradition of M. Bloch and the Annales school. Volume one: demographic and cognitive structure, e.g., occupation of space and cellularization,

and a bibliography of 1,054 items. Volume two: social and economic structure, particularly the seigneurie and the "féodalité."

53. Helle, Knut, "Norway in the High Middle Ages: Recent Views on the Structure of Society," Scandinavian Journal of History, 6(1981), 161-89.
    A review of research since World War II on the social formation of Norway in the twelfth and thirteenth centuries that discusses the extent of settlement, size of population, agricultural systems, patterns of land ownership, economic basis of the monarchy, and the political system. Notes a heavy influence of Marxist interpretations on the historiography of medieval Norway.

54. Holt, James C., "Feudal Society in Early Medieval England: I. The Revolution of 1066," Transactions of the Royal Historical Society, 5th ser., 32(1982), 193-212; "II. Notions of Patrimony," 33(1983), 193-220; "III: Patronage and Politics," 34(1984), 1-25.
    Explores notions of kinship and inheritance as practiced by Anglo-Saxons, imposed by Normans, and evolved during the twelfth century. Both social (i.e., local) and political (i.e., regional or national, and ultimately financial) aspects of the practices are considered.

55. I laici nella "societas christiana" dei secoli XI e XII: atti della terza Settimana internazionale di studio, Mendola, 1965 (Milan: Società editrice Vita e pensiero, 1968).
    Proceedings of a 1965 conference on the laity in the central Middle Ages. Leading papers by G. Duby on the laity and the Peace of God, E. Delaruelle on the religious culture of the laity in France, and G. Tellenbach on reformed monasticism and the laity. Most contributions are in French and the remainder are in Italian.

56. Parisse, Michel, Noblesse et chevalerie en Lorraine médiévale: les familles nobles du XIe au XIIe siècles (Nancy: Université de Nancy II, 1982).
    Concerned primarily with the lineage and genealogy of the Lorraine nobility but includes generalizations and notes trends to make the work of more than heraldic interest.

Included in this bibliography as an example of the better technical studies of family structure now being done on this period and for its bibliography of similar works.

57. Structures féodales et féodalisme dans l'occident méditerranéen (Xe-XIIIe siècles), bilan et perspectives de recherches: Colloque international, 1978 (Paris: Centre national de la recherche scientifique, 1980).

Thirty-seven papers include T. Bisson, "Feudalism in Twelfth-Century Catalonia" and H. Bresc, "Féodalité coloniale en terre d'Islam: la Sicile (1070-1240)."

58. Werner, Karl F., "Königtum und Fürstentum im französischen 12. Jahrhundert," in Probleme des 12. Jahrhunderts, Vorträge und Forschungen, 12 (Stuttgart: J. Thorbecke, 1968), 177-225. Translated by T. Reuter as "Kingdom and Principality in Twelfth-Century France" in T. Reuter, ed., Medieval Nobility: Studies on the Ruling Classes of France and Germany from the Sixth to the Twelfth Century (Amsterdam: North-Holland, 1979), 243-90.

Assesses the relationship between the principality and the monarchy from the principality's zenith during the reign of Philip I (1052-1108) at the beginning of the eleventh century through Philip Augustus's (1165-1223) domination of the principality at the close of the century. Examines the nature of the principality in light of the political, cultural, and royal administrative changes of the period.

2.1.1 Additional Works

59. Batany, Jean, "Norms, types et individus: la présentation des modèles sociaux au XIIème siècle," in D. Buschinger, ed., Littérature et société au moyen age: actes du Colloque des 5 et 6 mai 1978 (Paris, 1979), 177-200.
60. Bonenfant, Paul and G. Despy, "La noblesse en Brabant aux XIIe et XIIIe siècles," Moyen Age, 64(1958), 27-66.
61. Bonnassie, P., "Idéologie tripartite et révolution féodale," Moyen Age, 86(1980), 251-73.
62. Bosl, Karl, Herrscher und Beherrschte im deutschen Reich des 10.-12. Jahrhunderts (Munich: Bayerischen Akademie der Wissenschaft, 1963).

63. Bouchard, Constance B., "The Origins of the French Nobility: A Reassessment," American Historical Review, 86(1981), 501-32.
64. Cahen, Claude, "L'évolution sociale du monde musulman jusqu'an XIIe siècle face à celle du monde chrétien," Cahiers de civilisation médiévale, 1(1958), 451-63; 2(1959), 37-51.
65. Carpentier, Elisabeth, "Structures féodales et féodalisme dans l'Occident méditerranéen," Cahiers de civilisation médiévale, 26(1983), 141-46.
66. Dubled, Henri, "Recherches sur les dénominations de la seigneurie rurale et de ses dépendances aux XIe et XIIe siècles," Revue du moyen age latin, 12(1956), 241-96.
67. ------, "Noblesse et féodalité en Alsace du XIe au XIIIe siècle, Tijdschrift voor Rechtsgeschiedenis, 28(1960), 129-80.
68. Duby, Georges, "Structures de parenté et de noblesse: France du nord, XIe-XIIe siècles," in Miscellanea mediaevalia in memoriam Jan Frederik Niermeyer (Grőningen: J.B. Wolters, 1967), 149-65.
69. ------, "La féodalité? Une mentalité médiévale," Annales: économies, sociétés, civilisations, 13(1958), 765-71.
70. ------, "The Diffusion of Cultural Patterns in Feudal Society," Past and Present, 39(1968), 3-10.
71. Durand, Robert, Les campagnes portugaises entre Douro et Tage aux XIIe et XIIIe siècles (Paris: Centro cultural portugues, 1982).
72. Foreville, Raymonde, "The Synod of the Province of Rouen in the Eleventh and Twelfth Centuries," in C. Brooke et al., eds., Church and Government in the Middle Ages: Essays Presented to C.R. Cheney on His 70th Birthday (Cambridge, England: Cambridge University Press, 1976), 19-39.
73. Freed, John B., "Reflections on the Medieval German Nobility," American Historical Review, 91(1986), 553-75.
74. Genicot, Léopold, "Noblesse et principautés en Lotharingie du XIe au XIIIe siècle," Etudes sur les principautés lotharingiennes (Louvain: Bibliotheque de l'Université Leuven, 1975).
75. Guillemain, B., "L'histoire religieuse du Languedoc à la fin du XIIe siècle et au début du XIIIe," Annales du Midi, 83(1971), 101-17.

76. Hellmann, Manfred, "Wandlungen im staatlichen Leben Altrusslands und Polens während des 12. Jahrhunderts," in Probleme des 12. Jahrhunderts, Vorträge und Forschungen, 12 (Stuttgart: J. Thorbecke, 1968), 273-89.
77. Herlihy, David, "Land, Family and Women in Continental Europe, 701-1200," Traditio, 18(1962), 89-120.
78. Hollister, C. Warren, "The Irony of English Feudalism," Journal of British Studies, 2:2(May 1963), 1-26.
79. ------, "The Norman Conquest and the Genesis of English Feudalism," American Historical Review, 66(1960-61), 641-63.
80. Kammler, Hans, Die Feudalmonarchien: politische und wirtschaftlich-soziale Faktoren ihrer Entwicklung und Funktionsweise (Cologne: Böhlau, 1974).
81. Kumlien, Kjell, "Mission und Kirchenorganisation zur Zeit der Christianisierung Schwedens," in Probleme des 12. Jahrhunderts, Vorträge und Forschungen, 12 (Stuttgart: J. Thorbecke, 1968), 291-307.
82. Le Goff, Jacques, "Note sur société tripartie idéologie monarchique et renouveau économique dans la Chrétienté du IXe au XIIe siècle," Pour un autre moyen age: temps, travail, et culture en occident: 18 essais (Paris: Gallimard, 1977), 80-90. Translated by A. Goldhammer as "A Note on Tripartite Society, Monarchical Ideology, and Economic Renewal in Ninth- to Twelfth-Century Christendom," Time, Work, & Culture in the Middle Ages (Chicago: University of Chicago Press, 1980), 53-57.
83. Lemarignier, Jean F. et al., "Monachisme et aristocratie: autour de Saint-Taurin d'Évreux et du Bec (Xe-XIIIe siècles)," in L. Musset, ed., Aspects du monachisme en Normandie (IVe-XVIIIe siècles): actes du Colloque scientifique de l'"Année des abbayes normandes," Caen, 1979 (Paris: J. Vrin, 1982), 91-108.
84. Le Patourel, John H., Norman Barons (Bexhill-on-Sea: Historical Association, 1966).
85. Leyser, K. J., "The German Aristocracy from the Ninth to the Early Twelfth Century: A Historical and Cultural Sketch," Past and Present, 41(1968), 25-53.
86. Lyon, Bryce D., From Fief to Indenture: The Transition from Feudal to Non-Feudal Contract in Western Europe (Cambridge, MA: Harvard University Press, 1957).

87. Manteuffel, Tadeusz, The Formation of the Polish State: The Period of Ducal Rule, 963-1194 (Detroit: Wayne State University Press, 1982).
88. Newman, Charlotte A., "Family and Royal Favour in Henry I's England," Albion, 14(1982), 292-306.
89. Newman, William M., Les seigneurs de Nesle en Picardie (XIIe-XIIIe siècle), leur chartes et leur histoire: étude sur la noblesse régionale ecclésiastique et laïque (Philadelphia: American Philosophical Society, 1971).
90. ------, Le personnel de la cathédrale d'Amiens, 1066-1306 (Paris: A. et J. Picard, 1972).
91. Ourliac, Paul, "Les villages de la région toulousaine au XIIe siècle," Etudes d'histoire du droit médiévale (Paris: J. Picard, 1979), 113-24.
92. ------, "Le pays de La Selve à la fin du XIIe siècle," Annales du Midi, 80(1968), 581-602.
93. Parisse, Michel, Noblesse et chevalerie en Lorraine médiévale: les familles nobles du XIe au XIIIe siècle, (Nancy: Université de Nancy II, 1982).
94. Pastor de Togneri, Renya, "Historia de las familias en Castilla y Leon (siglos X-XIV) y su relacion con la formacion de los grandes dominios eclesiasticos," Cuadernos de historia de España, 43-44(1967), 88-118.
95. Poly, Jean P. and E. Bournazel, La mutation féodale (Xe-XIIe siècles) (Paris: Presses universitaires de France, 1980).
96. Poole, Austin L., Obligations of Society in the XIIth and XIIIth Centuries (Oxford: Clarendon Press, 1946).
97. Prestwich, J. O., "Anglo-Norman Feudalism and the Problem of Continuity," Past and Present, 26(1963), 39-57.
98. Richard, Jean, "Le château dans la structure féodale de la France de l'Est au XIIème siècle," in Probleme des 12. Jahrhunderts, Vorträge und Forschungen, 12 (Stuttgart: J. Thorbecke, 1968), 169-76.
99. ------, "Châteaux, châtelains et vassaux en Bourgogne aux XIe et XIIe siècles," Cahiers de civilisation médiévale, 3(1960), 433-47.
100. Ruiz Domenec, J. E., "Systeme de parenté et théorie de l'alliance dans la société catalane (env. 1000-env. 1240," Revue historique, 262(1979), 305-26.
101. Stenton, Frank M., The First Century of English Feudalism, 1066-1166, 2d ed. (Oxford: Clarendon Press, 1961).

102. Strayer, Joseph R., "The Two Levels of Feudalism," in R. Hoyt, ed., Life and Thought in the Early Middle Ages (Minneapolis: University of Minnesota Press, 1967), 51-65.
103. ------, "Feudalism in Western Europe," in R. Coulborn, ed., Feudalism in History (Princeton: Princeton University Press, 1956), 15-25.
104. Violante, Cinzio, "Nobiltà e chiese in Pisa durante i secoli XI e XII: il monasters di S. Matteo (prime richerche)," in J. Fleckenstein and K. Schmid, eds., Adel und Kirche: Gerd Tellenbach zum 65. Geburtstag dargebracht von Freunden und Schülern (Freiburg im Breisgau: Herder, 1968), 258-79.

2.1.1 Related Entries

Section 1.1: 8, 32; section 2.2: 165; section 2.3: 181; section 3.2: 327, 337, 339, 358; section 3.3: 403; section 4.1: 459; section 4.4.2: 690; section 4.5: 810.

2.1.2 Special Groups and Classes

105. Abels, Richard and E. Harrison, "The Participation of Women in Languedocian Catharism," Mediaeval Studies, 41(1979), 215-51.
Uses inquisition sources to ascertain the extent of female participation in Catharism, both as believers and perfects. Contrary to G. Koch (item 117) and H. Grundmann (item 174 in section 2.3), women participated in Languedocian Catharism in no greater proportion than in Catholicism. Begins with a good historiographical orientation to the problem.

106. Bouchard, Constance B., "The Structure of a 12th-Century French Family: The Lords of Seignelay," Viator, 10(1979), 39-56.
Questions "whether the modern term 'family' can justifiably be applied to twelfth-century groups of relatives, whether relatives used names to define the boundary of their group, what attempts were made to control the size of their group, and what were the relations between a family group and the Church."

107. Casey, Kathleen, "Women in Norman and Plantagenet England," in B. Kanner, ed., <u>The Women of England from Anglo-Saxon Times to the Present: Interpretive Bibliographical Essays</u> (Hamden, CN: Archon Books, 1979), 83-123.

>A bibliographic essay that covers over 225 books and articles, including much on the twelfth century in five broad categories: "Women's Work," "Life and Death," "Family Structures and the Concept of Domesticity," "The Unmarried State," and "The Cult of Love and the Marriage Debate." Summarizes important conclusions of leading works and adds many of the author's own interpretations.

108. Cohen, Jeremy, "Scholarship and Intolerance in the Medieval Academy: The Study and Evaluation of Judaism in European Christendom," <u>American Historical Review</u>, 91(1986), 592-613.

>Argues that twelfth- and thirteenth-century "methodological advances in Christian scholarship," "Christian pursuit of Hebraic scholarship and literalist exegesis of the Old Testament," and an "increasingly hostile ideological stance of the church toward the European Jewish community" contributed to a fundamental change in "Christian anti-Judaism" (p. 593). Cohen's study is limited to the religious texts of medieval scholars; an accompanying note by G. Langmuir (pp. 614-24) critiques Cohen's approach and offers comments from a social and economic perspective.

109. Dillard, Heath Portman, <u>Daughters of the Reconquest: Women in Castilian Town Society, 1100-1300</u> (Cambridge, England: Cambridge University Press, 1984).

>Uses royal charters (<u>fueros</u>) and other sources to assess the position and roles of women on the frontier of colonization in Christian Iberia. Based on the author's 1979 dissertation.

110. Duby, Georges and J. Le Goff, eds., <u>Famille et parenté dans l'occident médiéval: actes du Colloque de Paris, 1974</u> (Rome: Ecole francaise de Rome, 1977).

>A collection of 25 conference papers on the theme of familial structure and parentage in the Middle Ages. Several

deal principally with the twelfth century, and especially with Italy, such as C. Violante, "Quelques caractéristiques des structures familiales en Lombardie, Emilie et Toscane aux XIe et XIIe siècles" and G. Rossetti, "Histoire familiale et structures sociales et politiques à Pise aux XIe et XIIe siècles."

111. ------, "In Northwestern France: The 'Youth' in Twelfth-Century Aristocratic Society," in F. L. Cheyette, ed., <u>Lordship and Community in Medieval Europe: Selected Readings</u> (New York: Holt, Rinehart, and Winston, 1968), 198-209.

Aristocratic young men who were knighted but had not yet fully assumed the responsibilities of adulthood constituted a large, well-defined group occupying a tenuous social position. This <u>jeune</u> or <u>bachelier</u> in turn contributed to the romance model of the amorous relationship as it developed in the latter part of the twelfth century. Originally published as "Dans la France du nord-ouest, au XIIe siècle: les 'jeunes' dans la société aristocratique," <u>Annales: économies, sociétés, civilisations</u>, 19(1964), 835-46. See related item 726 in section 4.4.3.

112. ------, "An International Background: The Aristocratic Woman in France in the Twelfth Century," in N. Skyum-Nielsen and N. Lund, eds., <u>Danish Medieval History: New Currents</u> (Copenhagen: Museum Tusculanum Press, 1981), 57-68.

Focuses on women of the high aristocracy. Surveys sources, analyzes the prevailing system of values, and accounts for contradictions between values and appearances.

113. Duhamel-Amado, Claudie, "Une forme historique de la domination masculine: femme et mariage dans l'aristocratie Languedocienne à la fin du XIIe siècle," <u>Cahiers d'histoire de l'Institut de recherches marxistes</u>, 6(1981), 125-39.

Argues that women lost a substantial amount of social and economic freedom as society passed into a feudal mode of production that emphasized a patrilineal kinship system. Marriage provided the principal means by which men exercised control over women; through marriage women served as objects of exchange between patrilineal lines and as propagators of the lines, thereby politicizing their procreational function.

114. Gold, Penny Schine, The Lady & the Virgin: Image, Attitude, and Experience in Twelfth-Century France (Chicago: University of Chicago Press, 1985).
Assesses the depiction of women in both art and literature in the twelfth and thirteenth centuries, focusing chiefly on male attitudes and expressions. Concludes that images of women cannot readily be used as evidence regarding the status of women.

115. Hajdu, Robert, "The Position of Noblewomen in the Pays de Coutumes, 1100-1300," Journal of Family History, 5(1980), 122-44.
Legal sources, ecclesiastical charters, genealogical data, and feudal censuses form the basis for this quantitative study. Includes a helpful bibliography.

116. Herlihy, David, "The Making of the Medieval Family: Symmetry, Structure, and Sentiment," Journal of Family History, 8(1983), 116-30.
The twelfth and thirteenth centuries produced an agnatic or patrilineal kinship system (wherein ancestry was traced only through males) that supplanted but did not entirely replace the preceding cognatic and bilineal systems (wherein ancestry was traced through females or both females and males). For a broader consideration of this and related problems, see Herlihy's Medieval Households (Cambridge, MA: Harvard University Press, 1985).

117. Koch, Gottfried, Frauenfrage und Ketzertum im Mittelalter: die Frauenbewegung im Rahmen des Katharismus und des Waldensertums und ihre sozialen Wurzeln (12.-14. Jahrhundert) (Berlin: Akademie-Verlag, 1962).
Offers a controversial interpretation about the participation of women in heretical movevents during the central Middle Ages. Argues that women, especially of the minor noble and artisan classes, participated in the heresies in disproportionately large numbers owing to increasing socioeconomic discontent, a view critiqued by item 105. See also Koch's "Waldensertum und Frauenfrage im

Mittelalter," Forschungen und Fortschritte, 36(1962), 22-26; and "Die Frau in Mittelalterlichen Katharismus und Waldensertum," Studi medievali, 5(1964), 741-74.

118. McCrillis, Leon N., "The Demonization of Minority Groups in Christian Society during the Middle Ages." Ph.D. dissertation: University of California, Riverside, 1974.

   A marked increase in the demonization of Jews, heretics, and "Islamic-Negroid types" occurred in a wide variety of literary and visual sources in the eleventh through thirteenth centuries. The author attributes this upsurge to pre-existing prejudices intensified by the crusades, and heretical and millenarian movements.

119. McLaughlin, Mary M., "Peter Abelard and the Dignity of Women: Twelfth-Century 'Feminism' in Theory and Practice," Pierre Abélard, Pierre le Vénérable: les courants philosophiques, littéraires et artistiques en occident au milieu du XIIe siècle. Colloques internationaux du Centre national de la recherche scientifique, 1972 (Paris: Centre national de la recherche scientifique, 1975), 287-333.

   Abelard (1079-1142) is singular among twelfth-century authors in his regard for the "dignity" of women. His discussions of the nature and destiny of women go far beyond the notions of his contemporaries to reveal "a genuinely 'evangelical' feminism."

120. McLaughlin, Mary M., "Survivors and Surrogates: Children and Parents from the Ninth to the Thirteenth Centuries," in L. DeMause, ed., The History of Childhood (New York: Psychohistory Press, 1974), 101-81.

   A bibliographic gold mine. The chronological span is long and the author's interests range widely, but she has much to say on the eleventh and twelfth centuries. Includes extensive notes that provide suggestive comments and an abundance of references.

121. Painter, Sidney, "The Family and the Feudal System in Twelfth Century England," Speculum, 35(1960), 1-16.

   Considers English family connections, feudal structure, and customary law while answering "two broad questions--

the effects of family relationships on the distribution of property and their influence on political and military activities."

122. Richardson, Henry G., The English Jewry under Angevin Kings (London: Methuen, 1960).
Focuses on institutional relationships, associating the settlement and distribution of Jews in England, financial and political affiliations, and taxation of Jews. Norman Jewry is briefly surveyed in a supplementary note.

123. Scholz, Bernhard W., "Hildegard von Bingen on the Nature of Woman," American Benedictine Review, 31(1980), 361-83.
Culls the writings of one of the most prominent women of the twelfth century, presenting her thoughts on the psychology of women, their subjection to men, the complimentarity of woman and man, and female sexuality.

2.1.2 Additional Works

124. Bolton, Brenda M., "Vitae matrum: A Further Aspect of the Frauenfrage," in D. Baker, ed., Medieval Women (Oxford: B. Blackwell, 1978), 253-73.
125. Connell, Charles W., "In a Different Voice: Héloise and the Self-Image of Women of the Twelfth Century," in C.H. Berman et al., eds., The Worlds of Medieval Women: Creativity, Influence, Imagination (Morgantown, WV: West Virginia University Press, 1985), 24-40.
126. Farmer, Sharon, "Persuasive Voices: Clerical Images of Medieval Wives," Speculum, 61(1986), 517-43.
127. Flint, Valerie I., "Anti-Jewish Literature and Attitudes in the Twelfth Century," Journal of Jewish Studies, 37(1986), 39-57, 183-205.
128. Gieysztor, Aleksander, "La femme dans les civilisations des Xe-XIIIe siècles: la femme en Europe orientale," Cahiers de civilisation médiévale, 20(1977), 189-200.
129. Grabois, Aryeh, "L'Abbaye de Saint-Denis et les Juifs sous l'abbatiat de Suger," Annales: économies, sociétés, civilisations, 24(1969), 1187-95.

130. Hamilton, Bernard, "Women in the Crusader States: The Queens of Jerusalem, 1100-90," in D. Baker, ed., Medieval Women (Oxford: B. Blackwell, 1978), 143-74.
131. Rabinowitz, Louis I., Social Life of the Jews of Northern France in the XII-XIV Centuries, 2d ed. (New York: Hermon Press, 1972).
132. Thompson, Sally, "The Problem of the Cistercian Nuns in the Twelfth and Early Thirteenth Century," in D. Baker, ed., Medieval Women (Oxford: B. Blackwell, 1978), 227-52.
133. Valerio, Adriana, La questione feminile nei secoli X-XII (Naples, 1983).
134. Werner, Ernst, "Das Bild des anderen: Antihumanismus und Intoleranz im 12. Jahrhundert," Zeitschrift für Geschichtswissenschaft, 34(1986), 877-91.

2.1.2 Related Entries

Section 2.1.1: 77; section 2.2: 140, 141, 155, 161, 165; section 3.3: 404; section 4.1: 477; section 4.2: 535; section 4.3.1: 544; section 4.4.1: 664; section 4.4.2: 674, 681; section 4.4.3: 743; section 4.5: 795, 799.

2.2 Social Customs and Conditions

135. Bienvenu, J.M., "Pauvreté, misères et charité en Anjou aux XIe et XIIe siècles," Moyen Age, 72(1966), 389-424; 73(1967), 5-34, 189-216.
    Details the causes of poverty and traces a notable change in attitudes toward poverty in the twelfth century, largely the result of a new spiritual consciousness and the development of lay charity.

136. Boase, Roger, The Origin and Meaning of Courtly Love (Totowa, NJ: Rowman and Littlefield, 1977).
    Surveys scholarship on courtly love from the sixteenth century to the present, then distinguishes between (and explains) theories on the origin and theories of courtly love. Contains a 27-page bibliography, including a

bibliographic overview of the subject. See section 4.4 for works on the literature of courtly love.

137. Brooke, Christopher N., "Marriage and Society in the Central Middle Ages," in R.B. Outhwaite, ed., Marriage and Society: Studies in the Social History of Marriage (London: Europa, 1981), 17-34.
   Focuses on the eleventh and twelfth centuries, approaching the topic in an anecdotal rather than conceptual fashion. Rich in secondary and primary (especially English) references.

138. Brooke, Rosalind and C. Brooke, Popular Religion in the Middle Ages: Western Europe, 1000-1300 (London: Thames and Hudson, 1984).
   A general account of the practice and understanding of religion by "ordinary" people. Chapters center on such topics as relics, the cults of saints, the laity and the Church, and the Bible. Bibliographic notes included for each chapter.

139. Couvreur, Gilles, "Pauvreté et droits des pauvres à la fin du XIIe siècle," in G. Couvreur et al., La pauvreté: des sociétés de pénurie à la société d'abondance (Paris: A. Fayard, 1964), 13-37.
   The works of Raoul (d. 1200), a theologian in Paris, and Hugoccio (d. 1210), a canonist in Bologna, are used to explore institutional regard for some forms of (mostly voluntary) poverty in this period, such as apostolic, communal, and fraternal poverty.

140. Duby, Georges, Medieval Marriage: Two Models from Twelfth-Century France, lectures translated by E. Forster (Baltimore: Johns Hopkins University Press, 1978).
   Approaches marriage as a concern of families in a sense much broader than the individuals and alliances involved. The title refers to the aristocratic and the ecclesiastical models, each serving interests that frequently opposed those of the other. Takes up themes pursued by two of his other works: item 141 and "The Matron and the Mis-Married

Woman: Perceptions of Marriage in Northern France circa 1100," in T. Ashton et al., eds., Social Relations and Ideas: Essays in Honour of R.H. Hilton (Cambridge, England: Cambridge University Press, 1983), 89-108.

141. Duby, Georges, Le chevalier, la femme et le prêtre: le mariage dans la France féodale (Paris: Hachette litterature generale, 1981). Translated by B. Bray as The Knight, the Lady, and the Priest: The Making of Modern Marriage in Medieval France (New York: Pantheon Books, 1983).

Duby continues his interest in the subject of marriage with this broadening of some themes introduced in item 140. Centers on the eleventh and twelfth centuries, analyzing the works or examples of Burchard of Worms (c. 965-1025), Guibert of Nogent (1064?-c. 1125), the royal family, the ruling families of Amboise and Guines, and others. An introduction by N. Davis and Duby's preface provide excellent bibliographic background, a survey of Duby's work on this topic, and an analysis of the study itself. For a review of this and two other works by Duby (including item 50), see R.I. Moore, "Duby's Eleventh Century," History, 69(February 1984), 36-49.

142. Flori, Jean, L'essor de la chevalerie, XIe-XIIe siècles (Geneva: Droz, 1986).

Analyzes terms, formulae, and rituals. Concludes the social position of milites steadily improved through the twelfth century and the ideology of chivalry strengthened in the later decades in response to challenges from the church, bourgeoisie, and others. This is a sequel to his L'idéologie du glaive: préhistoire de la chevalerie (Geneva: Droz, 1983).

143. Guth, Klaus, Guibert von Nogent und die hochmittelalterliche Kritik an der Reliquienverehung (Augsburg: Winfried-Verk, 1970).

Guibert of Nogent (1064?-c. 1125) and his Relics of the Saints are used to examine the practice of relic veneration in the twelfth century.

144. Harper-Bill, Christopher and R. Harvey, eds., The Ideals and Practice of Medieval Knighthood: Papers From the First and Second Strawberry Hill Conferences (Dover, NH: Boydell Press, 1986).
Papers on a variety of topics, ranging from S. North on literature ("The Ideal Knight as Presented in Some French Narrative Poems, c. 1090-c. 1240: An Outline Sketch") to I. Pierce on arms ("The Knight, His Arms and Armour in the Eleventh and Twelfth Centuries").

145. Holmes, Urban T., Daily Living in the Twelfth Century (Madison: University of Wisconsin Press, 1966).
Uses Alexander Neckam's (1157-1217) De nominibus utensilium as the foundation for a sketch of everyday life in late-twelfth-century England and France, with a concentration on London and Paris. First published in 1953.

146. Jaeger, C.S., The Origins of Courtliness: Civilizing Trends and the Formation of Courtly Ideals, 939-1210 (Philadelphia: University of Pennsylvania Press, 1985).
Studies the "civilizing process" of the early Middle Ages that culminated in the emergence of courtly literature and chivalric ethics. Principal among the civilizing influences were the ideal of the Roman statesman, the development of a courtier class, and education for court service. Extensive notes and substantial bibliography. See section 4.4 for works on the literature of courtly love.

147. Keen, Maurice, Chivalry (New Haven: Yale University Press, 1984).
Comprehensive assessment of chivalry as a cultural and social force. Extends well beyond the twelfth century, but provides models necessary for any social or cultural study of the period.

148. Leclercq, Jean, Monks on Marriage: A Twelfth-Century View (New York: Seabury Press, 1982).
Series of lectures delivered in 1979 that elaborate the attitudes and theological perspectives of a major force in shaping the ecclesiastical view of marriage.

149. Longère, Jean, "Pauvreté et richesse chez quelques prédicateurs durant la second moitié du XIIe siècle," in M. Mollat, ed., Etudes sur l'histoire de la pauvreté, 2 vols. (Paris: Publications de la Sorbonne, 1974), 1:255-73.
Analyzes the sermons of Peter Comestor (d. 1179), Alan of Lille (1128-1203), Stephen Langton (1150-1228), and others on the subjects of poverty, wealth, alms, and social classes. These preachers stress the virtue of spiritual poverty, counsel against the association of spiritual poverty with material poverty, and blame avarice as the root cause for problems related to wealth rather than the fact of wealth itself.

150. Moller, Herbert, "The Meaning of Courtly Love," Journal of American Folklore, 73(1960), 39-52.
Offers a Freudian interpretation of courtly love, arguing that the collective fantasy of a pre-Oedipal "fixation to an infantile mother image" was the psychological basis for this cultural phenomenon. See section 4.4 for works on the literature of courtly love.

151. Moore, John C., Love in Twelfth-Century France (Philadelphia: University of Pennsylvania Press, 1972).
A very general survey of the spiritual, courtly, and intellectual aspects of the subject.

152. Povertà e ricchezza nella spiritualità dei secoli XI e XII: convegni, 1967 (Todi: Prsso l'Academia Tudertina, 1969).
Nine papers from a 1967 conference, including E. Werner's "Armut und Reichtum in den Vorstellungen ost- und westkirchlicher Haereticker des 10.-12. Jahrhunderts," P. Classen's "Eschatologische Ideen und Armuts bewegungen im 11. und 12. Jahrhundert," and L. Little's "The Function of the Jews in the Commercial Revolution." The Classen article also is available in J. Fleckenstein, ed., Ausgewahlte Aufsätze von Peter Classen, Vorträge und Forschungen, 28 (Sigmaringen: J. Thorbecke, 1983), 307-26.

153. Sheehan, Michael M., "Choice of Marriage Partner in the Middle Ages: Development and Mode of Application of a Theory of

Marriage," Studies in Medieval and Renaissance History, 1(1978), 1-33.

Views the twelfth century as an important period in the development of an ecclesiastical theory of marriage. Both canon law and theology produced major syntheses that codified a theory of marriage and provided a basis for further discussion, while the institutional Church developed an administrative structure capable of enforcing its dictates.

154. Van Hoecke, Willy and A. Welkenhuysen, eds., Love and Marriage in the Twelfth Century (Louvain: Louvain University Press, 1981).

Fifteen colloquium papers on a variety of social, intellectual, and literary aspects of the topic. Most are narrowly focused; nearly all are in either French or German.

2.2 Additional Works

155. Bornstein, Diane, The Lady in the Tower: Medieval Courtesy Literature for Women (Hamden: Archon Books, 1983).
156. Brooke, Christopher N., "Gregorian Reform in Action: Clerical Marriage in England, 1050-1200," Cambridge Historical Journal, 12(1956), 1-21, 187-88.
157. Bumke, Joachim, Studien zum Ritterbegriff im 12. und 13. Jahrhundert, 2d ed. (Heidelberg: C. Winter, 1977). Translated by W.T.H. Jackson and E. Jackson as The Concept of Knighthood in the Middle Ages (New York: AMS Press, 1982).
158. Chandler, Victoria, "Politics and Piety: Influences on Charitable Donations during the Anglo-Norman Period," Revue bénédictine, 90(1980), 63-71.
159. Denomy, Alexander J., The Heresy of Courtly Love (New York: D.X. McMullen, 1947).
160. Duby, Georges, Que sait-on de l'amour en France au XIIe siècle (Oxford: Clarendon Press, 1983).
161. Miller, Robert P., "The Wounded Heart: Courtly Love and the Medieval Antifeminist Tradition," Women's Studies, 2(1974), 335-50.
162. Mundy, John H., "Charity and Social Work in Toulouse, 1100-1250," Traditio, 22(1966), 203-87.

163. Newman, Francis X., ed., The Meaning of Courtly Love (Albany: State University of New York Press, 1969).
164. Platelle, H., "Le problème du scandale: les nouvelles modes masculines aux XIe et XIIe siècles," Revue belge de philologie et d'histoire, 53(1975), 1071-96.
165. Searle, Eleanor, "Seigneurial Control of Women's Marriage: The Antecedants and Function of Merchet in England," Past and Present, 82(February 1979), 3-43. Replies by P. Brand (with P. Hyams) and R. Faith, and rejoinder by Searle in 99(May 1983).
166. Sigal, Pierre A., "Pauvreté et charité aux XIe et XIIe siècles d'après quelques textes hagiographiques," in M. Mollat, ed., Etudes sur l'histoire de la pauvreté, 2 vols. (Paris: Publications de la Sorbonne, 1974), 1:141-62.

2.2 Related Entries

Section 2.1.1: 68, 77, 100; section 2.1.2: 113, 120; section 2.3: 200; section 3.3: 404; section 4.1: 466, 480; section 4.2: 524.

2.3 Social and Religious Movements

167. Berkhout, Carl T. and J.B. Russell, Medieval Heresies: A Bibliography, 1960-1979 (Toronto: Pontifical Institute of Medieval Studies, 1981).
   Covers heretical movements (as opposed to individual heretics) in Western Europe from the eighth through the fifteenth centuries. Over 2,000 entries arranged in 17 categories, including several relevant to the twelfth century.

168. Bolton, Brenda M., The Medieval Reformation (London: Holmes & Meier, 1983).
   Argues for a twelfth-century reformation of a magnitude comparable to the sixteenth-century Protestant reformation. Synthesizes recent scholarship on the nature of the crisis, religious movements both inside and outside the Church, religious women, and institutional reaction. Includes a well-selected bibliography.

169. Bolton, Brenda M., "Paupertas Christi: Old Wealth and New Poverty in the Twelfth Century," Studies in Church History, 14(1977), 95-103.
   A review article that investigates the related problems of vita apostolica as a form of personal and social renewal, and poverty as a means of renovatio--issues associated with twelfth-century questions of orthodoxy and heresy.

170. ------, "Tradition and Temerity: Papal Attitudes to Deviants, 1159-1216," Studies in Church History, 9(1972), 79-91.
   Details papal responses, both active and reactive, to the religious movements of the period prior to the Fourth Lateran Council's (1215) policy of exclusion.

171. Borst, Arno, Die Katharer (Stuttgart: A. Hiersemann, 1953).
   Over 20 years of intensive research have followed, but this remains the leading monograph on the subject. A 58-page historiographical essay ranging from the eleventh century through the 1940s, and the sections on history, ritual and doctrine, and legacy of the Cathars remain useful. Item 185 incorporates more recent research but is neither as critical nor scholarly.

172. Estrada, Juan A., "Un caso histórico de movimientos por una Iglesia popular: los movimientos populares de los siglos XI y XII," Estúdios eclesiásticos, 54(1979), 171-200.
   A synthesis of secondary works that discusses the development of a popular church in the eleventh and twelfth centuries, the lost opportunity for far-reaching reform, and the consequences of this failure for the later history of the Church. Integration of church and society and a consequent secularization of the Church are important elements in these movements.

173. Gonnet, Giovanni and A. Molnar, Les Vaudois au Moyen Age (Turin: Claudiana editrice, 1974).
   The standard account of the Waldensians, a movement extending from the twelfth century to the present. Provides background with a survey of twelfth-century religious currents, then focuses in turn on Peter Waldo (d. 1216) and

the Poor of Lyons. Includes a bibliography of several hundred primary and secondary works.

174. Grundmann, Herbert, Religiöse Bewegungen im Mittelalter, expanded ed. (Hildesheim: G. Olms, 1961).
Much of Grundmann's work has been updated or superseded but this effort remains a classic to which homage must be paid by later scholars, making Religiöse Bewegungen valuable for a citation search. Originally published in 1935, the expanded edition of 1961 appends Grundmann's 1955 article, "Neue Beiträge zur Geschichte der religiöse Bewegungen im Mittelalter" (Archiv für Kulturgeschichte, 37[1955], 129-82).

175. ------, Bibliographie zur Ketzergeschichte des Mittelalters (1900-1966) (Rome: Edizioni di storia e letteratura, 1967).
Grundmann makes available the bibliographic foundation for the studies cited in item 174. Nearly 800 entries are grouped in 15 categories, including sections on the eleventh and twelfth centuries and the major heretical movements.

176. Herlihy, David, "Alienation in Medieval Culture and Society," in F. Johnson, ed., Alienation: Concept, Term, and Meanings (New York: Seminar Press, 1973), 125-40.
Explores the dynamics of social alienation as they relate to the dissident social and religious movements of the central and later Middle Ages. Looks at changing demographics and familial structure as contributors to these developments.

177. Le Goff, Jacques, ed., Hérésies et sociétés dans l'europe préindustrielle, 11e-18e siècles (Paris: Mouton, 1968).
Thirty articles comprise this collection, nearly a third of which are relevant to the twelfth century. Papers include M. Chenu, "Orthodoxie et hérésie, le point de vue du théologien," M. Foucault, "Les déviations religieuses et le savoir médical," C. Thouzellier, "Tradition et résurgence dans l'hérésie médiévale," and C. Violante, "Hérésies urbaines et hérésies rurales in Italie du 11e au

13e siècle." G. Duby provides a conclusion and H. Grundmann contributes a 761-item bibliography.

178. Lourdaux, W. and D. Verhelst, eds., The Concept of Heresy in the Middle Ages (11th-13th c.): Proceedings of the International Conference, Louvain, 1973 (Louvain: Louvain University Press, 1976).

Eleven essays explore contemporary definitions of and regard for heresy. Contributions include R. Moore, "Heresy as a Disease" and J. Leclercq, "L'hérésie d'après les écrits de S. Bernard de Clairvaux."

179. Manselli, Raoul, Il secolo XII: religione popolare ed eresia (Rome: Jouvence, 1983).

Mostly reprints of earlier studies in twelfth-century popular religion--on Peter of Bruys (d. c. 1140), the Petrobruysians, the notions of Christianitas, for example--but also some new work on popular religiosity and intolerance.

180. Moore, R.I., The Origins of European Dissent (London: B. Blackwell, 1977).

Studies the social context of popular heresy in the eleventh and twelfth centuries, stressing the complexity of the movements and exploring their social dynamics. Also see Moore's "The Origins of Medieval Heresy," History, 55(1970), 21-36.

181. Nelson, Janet L., "Society, Theodicy and the Origins of Heresy: Towards a Reassessment of the Mediaeval Evidence," Studies in Church History, 9(1972), 65-77.

Theodicy is a state of crisis that occurs when extensive social change taxes a belief system's ability to accommodate new social situations. Some participants respond with expressions of greater piety within the belief system and others react in an anti-structural fashion by going outside the system. Twelfth-century heresies followed the latter response, which served to make still more intransigent an increasingly inflexible institutional Church.

182. Russell, Jeffrey B., "Interpretations of the Origins of Medieval Heresy," Mediaeval Studies, 25(1963), 26-53.
Explores the beginnings of Western heresy in the eighth through eleventh centuries, surveying major interpretations and schools of thought on the question from the mid-nineteenth century to the present.

183. Thouzellier, Christine, Catharisme et Valdéisme en Languedoc à la fin du 12e au début du 13e siècle, 2d ed. (Paris: Beatrice-Nauwelaerts, 1969).
Focuses on the polemical literature of the period while narrating and analysing the development of Catharism and Waldensianism in their early strongholds, as well as the orthodox reaction to them. Contains a substantial bibliography of primary and secondary works. See the author's Hérésie et hérétiques: Vaudois, Cathares, Patarins, Albigeois (Rome: Edizioni di storia e letteratura, 1969) for a collection of related articles that predate Catharisme et Valdéisme.

184. ------, "Hérésie et pauvreté à la fin du XIIe et au début du XIIIe siècle," in M. Mollat, ed., Études sur l'histoire de la pauvreté, 2 vols. (Paris: Publications de la Sorbonne, 1974), 1:371-88.
Uses Peter Waldo (d. 1216) and the Poor of Lyons to analyze the doctrinal and social problems associated with late-twelfth-century voluntary and involuntary poverty. Recounts Innocent III's (pope, 1198-1216) regard for these issues and demonstrates how the Poor of Lyons and similar movements paved the way for the more institutionally acceptable "poverty" movements of Dominic and Francis.

185. Wakefield, Walter L., Heresy, Crusade and Inquisition in Southern France, 1100-1250 (Berkeley: University of California Press, 1974).
A general survey that integrates social, political, and religious approaches to the problem of heresy in southern France. Discusses the origins of heresy and closely examines Cathars, Waldensians, and Languedocian society as a whole. Somewhat less authoritative than item 171 but

still valuable as a more recent synthesis of a broad spectrum of research.

186. Walther, Daniel, "A Survey of Recent Research on the Albigensian Cathari," Church History, 34(1965), 146-77.
    Overview of scholarship up to 1965 on Catharism and to a lesser extent on twelfth-century heresy in general. Points out major areas of study still deserving of attention, then lists and briefly discusses works under the headings "Bibliographical Essays," "Catharist Documents," and "Secondary Sources."

2.3 Additional Works

187. Berger, David, "Christian Heresy and Jewish Polemic in the Twelfth and Thirteenth Centuries," Harvard Theological Review, 68(1975), 287-303.
188. Brooke, Christopher N., "Heresy and Religious Sentiment, 1000-1250," Medieval Church and Society: Collected Essays (London: Sidgwick and Jackson, 1971), 139-61.
189. Cohn, Norman, The Pursuit of the Millenium, rev. and expanded ed. (Oxford: Oxford University Press, 1970).
190. Dossat, Yves, "L'hérésie en Champagne aux XIIe et XIIIe siècles," Eglise et hérésie en France au XIIIe (London: Variorum Reprints, 1982), essay 11.
191. Duvernoy, Jean, Le Catharisme, 2 vols. (Toulouse: E. Privat, 1976-79).
192. ------, "La religion cathare en Occitanie," in R. Lafont, ed., Les Cathares en Occitanie (Paris: A. Fayard, 1982), 199-262.
193. Fearns, James, "Peter von Bruis und die religiöse Bewegung des 12. Jahrhunderts," Archiv für Kulturgeschichte, 48(1966), 311-35.
194. Fossier, Robert, "Remarques sur l'étude des 'commotions' sociales aux XIe et XIIe siècles," Cahiers de civilisation médiévale, 16(1973), 45-50.
195. Frugoni, Arsenio, Arnaldo di Brescia nelle fonti del secolo XII (Rome: Istituto storico italiano per il Medio Evo, 1954).

196. Genicot, Léopold, "L'érémitisme du XIe siècle dans son contexte économique et social," in L'Eremitismo in occidente nei secoli XI e XII; atti della seconda Settimana internazionale di studio, Mendola, 1962 (Milan: Società editrice Vita e pensiero, 1965), 45-72.
197. Griffe, Elie, Les débuts de l'aventure cathare en Languedoc, 1140-1190 (Paris: Letouzey et Ane, 1969).
198. ------, Le Languedoc cathare de 1190 à 1210 (Paris: Letouzey et Ane, 1971).
199. Herbers, Klaus, Der Jakobuskult des 12. Jahrhunderts und der 'Liber sancti Jacobi' (Wiesbaden: F. Steiner, 1984).
200. Jalby, Robert, "Des rites et pratiques attribués aux hérétiques (XIe-XIIIe siècles)," Revue du Tarn, 110(1983), 135-46.
201. ------, "Grundzüge der religösen Geschichte Italiens im 12. Jahrhundert," Vorträge und Forschungen. Sonderheft, 9(1971), 5-35.
202. Manselli, Raoul, L'eresia del male, 2d ed. (Naples: Morano, 1980).
203. Martini, Magda, Pierre Valdo, le Pauvre de Lyon: l'épopée vaudoise (Geneva: Labor et fides, 1961).
204. Moore, R. I., "Popular Violence and Popular Heresy in Western Europe, c. 1000-1179," Studies in Church History, 21(1984), 43-50.
205. Niel, Fernand, Albigeois et Cathares, 9th ed. (Paris: Presses universitaires de France, 1979).
206. Runciman, Steven, The Medieval Manichee: A Study of Christian Dualist Heresy (Cambridge, England: Cambridge, 1947).
207. Santini, Luigi, De Pierre Valdo à l'église vaudoise (Geneva: Labor et fides, 1974).
208. Toubert, Pierre, "Hérésies et réforme ecclésiastique en Italie aux XIe et au XIIe siècles: à propos de deux études recentes," Revue des etudes italiennes, 8(1961), 58-71.
209. Vaudois languedociens et pauvres catholiques (Toulouse: E. Privat, 1967).
210. Vinay, T., "Die Waldenser," in H.J. Schultz, Die Wahrheit der Ketzer (Stuttgart: Kreuz, 1968), 60-71, 250-60.
211. Wild, Georg, Bogumilen und Katharer in ihrer Symbolik (Wiesbaden: F. Steiner, 1970).

2.3 Related Entries

<u>Section 2.1.2</u>: 105, 120; <u>section 2.2</u>: 152; <u>section 4.1</u>: 458, 459, 462, 481; <u>section 4.3.2</u>: 582.

3.0 POLITICS, GOVERNMENT, AND ARMED CONFLICT

3.1 National Monarchies and the Church

England

212. Alexander, James W., "A Historiographical Survey: Norman and Plantagenet Kings Since World War II," Journal of British Studies, 24(1985), 94-109.
　　Lists source material published since 1945, then proceeds chronologically by king, enumerating and evaluating noteworthy (but by no means only good) biographies. Includes a bibliography arranged by year of publicaton.

213. ------, "The Becket Controversy in Modern Historiography," Journal of British Studies, 9(May 1970), 1-26.
　　Discusses many aspects of the conflict between Henry II (1133-1189) and Thomas Becket (1118-1170) and reviews leading scholarship on these questions, providing both intellectual and bibliographic frameworks for further considerations of the controversy. See related item 551 in section 4.3.1.

214. Altschul, Michael, Anglo-Norman England, 1066-1154 (London: Cambridge University Press, 1969).

A bibliography that covers many subject areas with the bulk of the 1,838 citations falling in the chapters on constitutional and administrative history, political history, and foreign relations. Sections are subdivided by such categories as printed sources, surveys, monographs, biographies, and articles.

215. Barlow, Frank, William Rufus (Berkeley: University of California Press, 1983).
A noncontroversial biography of a controversial monarch. Included largely for its sizable recent bibliography.

216. Callahan, Thomas, "The Notion of Anarchy in England, 1135-1154: A Bibliographical Survey," British Studies Monitor, 62(Spring 1976), 23-35.
An overview of historical research on this era, focusing on the historiographical schools of the nineteenth and twentieth centuries.

217. Cantor, Norman F., Church, Kingship, and Lay Investiture in England, 1089-1135 (Princeton: Princeton University Press, 1958).
Studies both the ideological and political aspects of the conflict in England and on the continent. The failure of Anselm (1033-1109) and Urban II (1042-1199) to extend the Gregorian Reform to England and thereby undermine the Norman system of church-state governance was of greater significance for the English Church than the dispute between Henry II and Thomas Becket.

218. Cheney, Christopher R., Hubert Walter (London: T. Nelson & Sons, 1967).
Emphasizes the ecclesiastical aspects of Hubert Walter's (d. 1205) life. C. Young, Hubert Walter, Lord of Canterbury and Lord of England (Durham, NC, 1968) stresses the royal administrative aspects.

219. Cheney, Mary G., Roger, Bishop of Worcester, 1164-1179 (Oxford: Clarendon Press, 1980).
Goes well beyond the subject himself to provide insight into the nature of the high-level politics of the time.

Best read in company with the biographies of Henry II (W. Warren) and Thomas Becket (D. Knowles).

220. Chibnall, Marjorie, Anglo-Norman England, 1066-1166 (New York: B. Blackwell, 1986).
A broad survey and a synthesis of recent scholarly work. Well-noted; good bibliography.

221. Douglas, David C., The Norman Fate, 1100-1154 (Berkeley: University of California Press, 1976).
Sequel to the author's William the Conqueror (1964) and The Norman Achievement, 1050-1100 (1969). Surveys the Norman presence in England, Normandy, and Sicily, and assesses its impact on European politics. Includes a good bibliography.

222. Foreville, Raymonde, Thomas Becket dans la tradition historique hagiographique (London: Variorum Reprints, 1981).
Sixteen of the many articles produced by an eminent Becket scholar during more than forty years of research. Three sections: "Tradition historique," "Tradition hagiographique," and "Perspectives théologiques." See related item 551 in section 4.3.1.

223. Gillingham, John, The Angevin Empire (London: E. Arnold, 1984).
Stresses the distinctiveness of the Angevin Empire as compared to its Norman predecessor. A bibliographical note provides a thorough and recent bibliography.

224. Hollister, C. Warren, "Normandy, France, and the Anglo-Norman regnum," Monarchy, Magnates and Institutions in the Anglo-Norman World (London: Hambledon Press, 1986), 17-57.
Normandy and England were governed as one kingdom under one monarch rather than as a duchy and a kingdom ruled by one person who alternated in the roles of duke and king. The author independently arrived at this conclusion at the same time as J. Le Patourel, item 231 below. Originally published in Speculum, 51(1976), 202-42.

225. Hollister, C. Warren, "War and Diplomacy in the Anglo-Norman World: The Reign of Henry I," Monarchy, Magnates and Institutions in the Anglo-Norman World (London: Hambledon Press, 1986), 273-89.
> Begins with the premise that the financial needs of war and diplomacy largely determined the institutional and constitutional history of England, then argues that issues of war and peace greatly influenced Norman fiscal policy (as well as other policies) and that Norman diplomatic concerns were more international than historians have generally believed. Originally published in Anglo-Norman Studies (Proceedings of the Battle Conference on Anglo-Norman Studies), 6(1984 for 1983), 72-88.

226. ------ and T.K. Keefe, "The Making of the Angevin Empire," Monarchy, Magnates and Institutions in the Anglo-Norman World (London: Hambledon Press, 1986), 247-71.
> Further development of the thesis of a cautious Anglo-Norman kingdom followed by an Angevin empire more willing to take risks, as sketched in item 224. Originally published in Journal of British Studies, 12(May 1973), 1-25. The concept of an Angevin empire is further discussed by B. Bachrach, "The Idea of the Angevin Empire," Albion, 10(1978), 293-99.

227. ------, "Henry I and the Invisible Transformation of Medieval England," Monarchy, Magnates and Institutions in the Anglo-Norman World (London: Hambledon Press, 1986), 303-15.
> Reviews both contemporary and modern assessments of Henry I (1068-1135). Concludes Henry's true legacy lies not so much in specific accomplishments as in seeking traditional ends through new means, a characteristic of the twelfth century generally. Originally published in H. Mayr-Harting and R.I. Moore, eds., Studies in Medieval History Presented to R.H.C. Davis (London: Hambledon Press, 1985), 119-31.

228. Jolliffe, J.E., Angevin Kingship, 2d ed. (London: A. and C. Black, 1963).
> Examines the growth of royal power in the latter part of the twelfth century, the nature and origin of that power, and the means used to exercise it.

229. Kealey, Edward J., "Recent Writing about Anglo-Norman England," <u>British Studies Monitor,</u> 9(1979), 3-22.
    Bibliographies and other reference works, festschriften, text editions and translations, biographies, monographs, and journal articles are enumerated and briefly discussed.

230. Knowles, David, <u>Thomas Becket</u> (London: A. & C. Black, 1971).
    A sympathetic but fair assessment of Becket (1118-1170) and the so-called Becket controversy. See related item 551 in section 4.3.1.

231. Le Patourel, John H., <u>The Norman Empire</u> (Oxford: Clarendon Press, 1976).
    Argues for the political unity of the Anglo-Norman realm, a viewpoint contrary to what was at the time of publication the prevailing view of England and Normandy as distinct political units. Useful bibliography included. See item 224 for a similar perspective.

232. Newman, Charlotte A., "Henry I's Old and New Men: Social History and Prosopography," <u>Medieval Prosopography,</u> 1(1980), 35-43.
    A bibliographic essay that centers on the value of comparative biography for historians of early twelfth-century England. Discusses works by R. Southern, J. Le Patourel, C. Hollister, and others.

233. Warren, Wilfred L., <u>Henry II</u> (Berkeley: University of California Press, 1973).
    The leading scholarly biography of this monarch. Includes a very good bibliography. See J. Schlight, <u>Henry II Plantagenet</u> (New York: Twayne Publishers, 1973) for a less studious account.

France

234. Bautier, Robert H., ed., <u>La France de Philippe Auguste; le temps de mutation: actes du Colloque international, Paris, 1980</u> (Paris: Centre national de la recherche scientifique, 1982).
    Fifty papers presented to a 1980 conference include sections on "Le roi et son image," "Le royaume, le domaine

et la politique royale," and "Le roi, l'église et la croisade," with papers by R. Bautier ("Philippe Auguste: la personalité du roi"), J. Boussard ("Philippe Auguste et les Plantagenêts"), and B. Guillemain ("Philippe Auguste et l'épiscopat").

235. Dunbabin, Jean, <u>France in the Making, 843-1180</u> (Oxford: Oxford University Press, 1985).
Largely a political narrative that chronicles the gradual emergence of a sense of (political) community. Chapters on sources, appendixes on genealogical tables and recommended reading.

236. Fawtier, Robert, <u>Les Capétiens et la France: leur rôle dans sa construction</u> (Paris: Presses universitaires de France, 1942). Translated by L. Butler as <u>The Capetian Kings of France: Monarch and Nation, 987-1328</u> (London: Macmillan, 1960).
Remains the leading account of the kingdom of France in the central Middle Ages. Devotes much attention to the Capetians and their advisers with less attention paid to Capetian administration and institutions. See related item 237.

237. Hallam, Elizabeth M., <u>Capetian France, 987-1328</u> (London: Longman, 1980).
Straightforward, chronological narration of the monarchy and national political institutions. Compare item 236, which takes a topical approach to the same material.

238. Pacaut, Marcel, <u>Louis VII et son royaume</u> (Paris: S.E.V.P.E.N., 1964).
A scholarly though general survey of this French king and his kingdom--virtually the only substantial consideration of Louis VII and France.

Germany

239. Dobozy, Maria, "The Theme of the Holy War in German Literature, 1152-1190: Symptom of Controversy Between Empire and Papacy?" <u>Euphorion</u>, 80(1986), 341-62.

Investigates late-twelfth-century German epics, especially Müncher Oswald and Orendel, for content related to the crusades. Concludes these works reflect an "assertive imperial policy and the increasingly political and nationalistic goal of the crusades themselves." (p. 343)

240. Fuhrmann, Horst, Deutsche Geschichte im hohen Mittelalter, 2d ed. (Göttingen: Vandenhoeck und Ruprecht, 1983). Translated by T. Reuter as Germany in the High Middle Ages (Cambridge, England: Cambridge University Press, 1986).
Largely a political narrative of German national politics from Henry III (1017-1056) to Henry VI (1165-1197), though tempered with references to social and economic matters and often placed in a European context. In the English version, Fuhrmann's original notes and bibliography are replaced with a bibliography by the translator.

241. Jordan, Karl, "Staufer und Kapetinger im 12. Jahrhundert," Francia, 2(1974), 136-51.
A comparative study of the German and French monarchies during the twelfth century: The Investiture Contest, feudalization of the Church, influence of the English kings, and relations between the French and Germans themselves.

242. Koch, Gottfried, Auf dem Wege zum "sacrum imperium": Studien zur ideologischen Herrschaftsbegründung der deutschen Zentralgewalt im 11. und 12. Jahrhundert (Graz: Böhlau, 1972).
Articulates the ideological bases of German kingship in the central Middle Ages, focusing on the principle of divine mandate, ancient and Germanic traditions, and royal and ecclesiastical legal formulations. Contains a sizable bibliography.

243. Manselli, Raoul and J. Riedmann, eds., Federico Barbarossa nel dibattito storiografico in Italia e in Germania (Bologna: Il Mulino, 1982).
Papers from a 1980 symposium of several leading Barbarossa scholars. Collectively, the papers present a revised, sympathetic view of Barbarossa's (1123-1190) motivations and intentions. All papers are in Italian.

244. Munz, Peter, *Frederick Barbarossa: A Study in Medieval Politics* (Ithaca: Cornell University Press, 1969).
   A kinder view of Barbarossa (1123-1190) than many historians have offered, viewing the emperor as one who adapted well to new situations. Provides good access to the scholarly (especially German) literature on Barbarossa.

245. Opll, Ferdinand, *Stadt und Reich im 12. Jahrhundert (1125-1190)* (Vienna: Böhlau, 1986).
   Analyses of the relations between the imperial administration and 106 German, Italian, and Burgundian municipalities. A detailed and careful study of imperial power vis-à-vis the cities, stopping short of generalizations or conclusions.

Other and General

246. Angold, Michael, *The Byzantine Empire, 1025-1204: A Political History* (London: Longman, 1985).
   While essentially a political history, this survey also includes chapters on major economic, social, and intellectual currents. The work's chief value is as a general and bibliographic orientation to twelfth-century Byzantium.

247. Baldwin, Marshall W., *Alexander III and the Twelfth Century* (Glen Rock, NJ: Newman Press, 1968).
   Goes beyond a narrow biography of Alexander (pope, 1159-1181) to include assessments of the papal election of 1159, international politics, and the Becket controversy.

248. Benson, Robert L., "Political *renovatio*: Two Models from Roman Antiquity," in R. Benson and G. Constable, eds., *Renaissance and Renewal in the Twelfth Century* (Cambridge, MA: Harvard University Press, 1982), 339-86.
   Traces the uses and gauges the implications of the twelfth-century revival (*renovatio*) of two political models from Antiquity: the Roman commune's notion of senate and Frederick Barbarossa's (1123-1190) concept of empire. Includes a bibliographical note.

249. Brand, Charles M., Byzantium Confronts the West, 1180-1204 (Cambridge, MA: Harvard University Press, 1968).

Synthesizes a large body of research on the relations between Byzantium and Western Europe in the decades prior to the capture of Constantinople by the Fourth Crusade. Copious notes and an extensive bibliography, though somewhat dated. See related item 542 in section 4.3.1.

250. Chodorow, Stanley A., Christian Political Theory and Church Politics: The Ecclesiology of Gratian's "Decretum" (Berkeley: University of California Press, 1972).

Analyzes Gratian's (d. c. 1179) works, especially the Decretum, to reconstruct the canonist's ecclesiological world view. Argues that Gratian provided the theoretical foundation for a post-Gregorian reform party.

251. Deér, József, Papsttum und Normannen: Untersuchungen zu ihren lehnsrechtlichen und kirchenpolitischen Beziehungen (Cologne: Böhlau, 1972).

Explores feudal relations between the papacy and the Normans in southern Italy during the eleventh and twelfth centuries. Earlier chapters consider the origins of the Norman-papal conflict and argue that the papacy first entered into feudal relationships with secular princes in southern Italy; later chapters analyze the nature and consequences of the conflict.

252. Jakobs, Hermann, Kirchenreform und Hochmittelalter, 1046-1215 (Munich: R. Oldenbourg, 1984).

A handbook on church reform during this period. Includes a narrative précis, a literature review, and a 1,054-item bibliography of primary and secondary sources.

253. Pacaut, Marcel, Alexandre III: étude sur la conception du pouvoir pontifical dans sa pensée et dans son oeuvre (Paris: J. Vrin, 1956).

Assesses the influence of Alexander's (pope, 1159-1181) legal training (including extensive instruction from Gratian) on his conception of papal institutions and power, and the extent to which these views in turn shaped papal policy toward various European states, particularly the Empire.

254. Pennington, Kenneth, <u>Pope and Bishops: The Papal Monarchy in the Twelfth and Thirteenth Centuries</u> (Philadelphia: University of Pennsylvania Press, 1984).

Explores the theoretical foundations for the development of papal power, concentrating on the thirteenth century but including much on the twelfth. Also contains a substantial and current bibliography.

255. <u>Probleme des 12. Jahrhunderts</u>, Vorträge und Forschungen, 12 (Stuttgart: J. Thorbecke, 1968).

Several noteworthy articles on national and international politics, including: F. Schmale, "Papsttum und Kurie zwischen Gregor VII. und Innocenz II." and "Lothar III. und Friedrich I. als Könige und Kaiser"; F. Hausmann, "Die Anfänge des staufischen Zeitalters unter Konrad III."; H. Büttner, "Friedrich Barbarossa und Burgund: Studien zur Politik der Staufer während des 12. Jahrhunderts"; K. Werner, "Königtum und Fürstentum in französischen 12. Jahrhundert"; and H. Beck, "Byzanz und der Westen im 12. Jahrhundert."

256. Runciman, Steven, <u>The Eastern Schism: A Study of the Papacy and the Eastern Churches during the XIth and XIIth Centuries</u> (Oxford: Clarendon Press, 1955).

The causes of the schism were several, broad, and took effect over many years--different ecclesiastical traditions, cultural differences (even animosity), the reformed papacy, Norman invasions of Byzantine holdings in Italy and Sicily, the crusades--rather than the result of particular events. See related item 542 in section 4.3.1.

257. Servatius, Carlo, <u>Paschalis II. (1099-1118): Studien zu seiner Person und seiner Politik</u> (Stuttgart: A. Hiersemann, 1979).

Paschal II (1099-1118) is the centerpiece of this study but it is sufficiently broad to prove valuable for any consideration of either the papacy as an institution or imperial-papal relations in the twelfth century.

3.1 Additional Works

England

258. Appleby, John T., England without Richard, 1189-1199 (Ithaca: Cornell University Press, 1965).
259. ------, "The Ecclesiastical Foundations of Henry II," Catholic Historical Review, 48(1962-63), 205-15.
260. Barber, Richard W., Henry Plantagenet: A Biography (London: Barrie and Rockliff with Pall Mall Press, 1964).
261. Barlow, Frank, The English Church, 1066-1154: A History of the Anglo-Norman Church (London: Longman, 1979).
262. ------, The Feudal Kingdom of England, 1042-1216 (London: Longman, 1955).
263. ------, Thomas Becket (London: Weidenfeld and Nicolson, 1986).
264. Bautier, Robert H., "'Empire Plantagenêt' ou 'espace Plantagenêt': y eut-il une civilisation du monde Plantagenêt?" Cahiers de civilisation médiévale, 29(1986), 139-47.
265. Boussard, Jacques, Le gouvernement d'Henri II Plantagenêt (Paris: Librarie d'Argences, 1956).
266. Cassady, Richard F., The Norman Achievement (London: Sidgwick & Jackson, 1986).
267. Cronne, Henry A., The Reign of Stephen, 1135-54: Anarchy in England (London: Weidenfeld and Nicholson, 1970).
268. Davis, Ralph H., King Stephen, 1135-1154 (Berkeley: University of California Press, 1967).
269. Duggan, Charles, "The Significance of the Becket Dispute in the History of the English Church," Canon Law in Medieval England: The Becket Dispute and Decretal Collections (London: Variorum Reprints, 1982), essay 1.
270. Gibson, Margaret T., Lanfranc of Bec (Oxford: Clarendon Press, 1978).
271. Gillingham, John, Richard the Lionheart (London: Weidenfeld and Nicholson, 1978).
272. ------, "The Art of Kingship: Richard I, 1189-99," History Today, 35(April 1985), 17-23.
273. Hollister, C. Warren, "Magnates and Curiales in Early Norman England," Monarchy, Magnates and Institutions in the Anglo-Norman World (London: Hambledon Press, 1986), 97-115. Originally published in Viator, 8(1977), 63-81.

274. Hollister, C. Warren, "Recent Trends in Anglo-Norman Scholarship: The New Political History," Albion, 14(1982), 254-57.
275. Holt, James C., "The End of the Anglo-Norman Realm," Proceedings of the British Academy, 61(1975), 223-65.
276. Kelly, Amy, Eleanor of Acquitaine and the Four Kings (Cambridge, MA: Harvard University Press, 1950).
277. Kibler, William W., ed., Eleanor of Aquitaine, Patron and Politician (Austin: University of Texas Press, 1976).
278. King, Edmund, "The Anarchy of King Stephen's Reign," Transactions of the Royal Historical Society, 5th ser., 34 (1984), 133-53.
279. Knowles, David, The Episcopal Colleagues of Archbishop Thomas Becket (Cambridge, England: Cambridge University Press, 1951).
280. Le Patourel, John H., Normandy and England, 1066-1144 (Reading: University of Reading Press, 1971). Reprinted in his Feudal Empires: Norman and Plantagenet (London: Hambledon Press, 1984).
281. ------, "The Norman Succession, 966-1135," English Historical Review, 86(1971), 225-50.
282. Leyser, K. J., "England and the Empire in the Early Twelfth Century," Transactions of the Royal Historical Society, 5th ser., 10(1960), 61-83.
283. Mayr-Harting, H., "Henry II and the Papacy, 1170-1189," Journal of Ecclesiastical History, 16(1965), 39-53.
284. Meade, Marion, Eleanor of Acquitaine: A Biography (New York: Hawthorn Books, 1977).
285. Morey, Adrian and C. Brooke, Gilbert Foliot and His Letters (Cambridge, England: Cambridge University Press, 1965).
286. Nicholl, Donald, Thurston, Archbishop of York (1114-1140) (York: Stonegate Press, 1964).
287. Pontal, Odette, "Les évêques dans le monde Plantagenêt," Cahiers de civilisation médiévale, 29(1986), 129-37.
288. Powicke, Frederick M., The Loss of Normandy, 1189-1204, 2d ed. (Manchester: Manchester University Press, 1961).
289. Saltman, Avrom, Theobald, Archbishop of Canterbury (London: University of London Press, 1956).
290. Southern, Richard W., "The Place of Henry I in English History," Proceedings of the British Academy, 48(1962), 127-69.

291. Southern, Richard W., "King Henry I," Medieval Humanism and Other Studies (Oxford: B. Blackwell, 1970), 206-33.
292. Spear, David S., "The Norman Episcopate Under Henry I, King of England and Duke of Normandy (1106-1135)." Ph.D. dissertation: University of California, Santa Barbara, 1982.
293. Turner, Ralph V., "Religious Patronage of the Angevin Royal Administrators, c. 1170-1239," Albion, 18(1986), 1-21.
294. Vaughn, Sally N., The Abbey of Bec and the Anglo-Norman State, 1034-1136 (Woodbridge, England: Boydell Press, 1981).
295. Warren, Wilfred L., King John (New York: W.W. Norton, 1961).

France

296. Petit-Dutaillis, C., La monarchie féodale en France et en Angleterre (Xe-XIIIe siècle) (Paris: La Renaissance du libre, 1936). Translated by E. Hunt as The Feudal Monarchy in France and England (London: K. Paul, Trench, Trubner & Co., 1936).

Germany

297. Engels, Odilo, "Beiträge zur Geschichte der Staufer im 12. Jahrhundert," Deutsches Archiv für Erforshung des Mittelalters, 27(1971), 373-456.
298. Haverkamp, Alfred, Aufbruch und Gestaltung: Deutschland, 1056-1273 (Munich: C. Beck, 1984).
299. Kienast, Walther, Deutschland und Frankreich in der Kaiserzeit (900-1270): Weltkaiser und Einzelkönige, 2d ed. (Stuttgart: Hiersemann, 1974-1975).
300. Leyser, Karl J., Medieval Germany and its Neighbours, 900-1250 (London: Hambledon Press, 1982).
301. Pacaut, Marcel, Frédéric Barberousse (Paris: A. Fayard, 1967). Translated by A. Pomerans as Frederick Barbarossa (New York: Scribner, 1970).
302. Planitz, Hans, Die deutsche Stadt im Mittelalter, 2d ed. (Graz: Böhlau, 1965).
303. Wolf, Gunther, ed., Friedrich Barbarossa (Darmstadt: Wissenschaftliche Buchgesettschaft, 1975).

304. Zielinski, H., Der Reichsepiskopat in spätottonischer und salischer Zeit (1002-1125) (Wiesbaden: F. Steiner, 1984).

Other and General

305. Cheney, Christopher R., The Papacy and England, 12th-14th Centuries (London: Variorum Reprints, 1982).
306. Foreville, Raymonde, Latran I, II, III et Latran IV (Paris: Editions de l'Orante, 1965).
307. Kantorowicz, Ernst H., The King's Two Bodies: A Study in Mediaeval Political Theology (Princeton: Princeton University Press, 1957).
308. Kennan, Elizabeth, "The De consideratione of St. Bernard of Clairvaux and the Papacy in the Mid-Twelfth Century: A Review of Scholarship," Traditio, 23(1967), 73-115.
309. Magdalino, Paul, "Aspects of 12th-Century Byzantine Kaiserkritik," Speculum, 58(1983), 326-46.
310. Maleczek, Werner, Papst und Kardinalskolleg von 1191 bis 1216: die Kardinale unter Coelestin III. und Innocenz III. (Vienna: Österreichischen Akademie der Wissenschaften, 1984).
311. Morrison, Karl F., Tradition and Authority in the Western Church (Princeton: Princeton University Press, 1969).
312. Pfaff, Volkert, "Der Widerstand der Bischöfe gegen den päpstlichen Zentralismus um 1200," Zeitschrift der Savigny-Stiftung für Rechtsgeschichte. Kanonistische Abteilung, 66(1980), 459-65.
313. ------, "Zur Geschichte des Papsttums von 1181 bis 1198," Zeitschrift der Savigny-Stiftung für Rechtsgeschichte Kanonistische Abteilung, 69(1983), 250-66.
314. Schlight, John, Monarchs and Mercenaries, 1066-1189 (New York: New York University Press, 1968).
315. Schmale, Franz J., Studien zum Schisma des Jahres 1130 (Cologne: Böhlau, 1961).
316. Southern, Richard W., "Pope Adrian IV," Medieval Humanism and Other Studies (Oxford: B. Blackwell, 1970), 234-52.
317. Steindorff, Ludwig, Die dalmatinischen Städte im 12. Jahrhundert: Studien zu ihrer politischen Stellung und gesellschaftlichen Einleitung (Cologne: Böhlau, 1984).
318. Tierney, Brian, Foundations of the Conciliar Theory: The Contribution of the Medieval Canonists from Gratian to the

Great Schism (Cambridge, England: Cambridge University Press, 1955).
319. Tillman, Helene, Papst Innocenz III. (Bonn: L. Rohrscheid, 1954). Translated by W. Sax as Pope Innocent III (Amsterdam: Elsevier North-Holland, 1980).
320. Le Troisième Concile de Latran (1179): sa place dans l'histoire. Communications présentées à la Table Ronde du CNRS, 1980 (Paris: Études augustiniennes, 1982).
321. Ullmann, Walter, The Growth of Papal Government in the Middle Ages: A Study in the Ideological Relation of Clerical to Lay Power (London: Methuen, 1965).

3.1 Related Entries

Section 2.1.1: 53, 73, 80, 84, 101; section 3.2: 322, 340, 347, 355; section 3.3: 365, 369, 373, 375, 377, 379, 383, 389, 393; section 3.4: 448, 450; section 4.2: 488; section 4.4.2: 687; section 4.4.3: 722.

3.2 Local and Regional Studies

322. Atti del Congresso internazionale di studi sulla Sicilia normanna, Palermo, 1972 (Palermo: Istituto di storia medievale, 1973).
    Proceedings include 25 papers that collectively constitute a recent synthesis on Norman Sicily. One paper is in French; all others are in Italian.

323. Barrow, G.W., The Anglo-Norman Era in Scottish History (Oxford: Oxford University Press, 1980).
    Studies English, French, and Flemish settlement patterns in lowland Scotland in the twelfth and thirteenth centuries. Concluding chapters compare the resulting Scottish strain of feudalism with its English parent.

324. Bisson, Thomas N., "L'essor de la Catalogne: identité, pouvoir et idéologie dans une société du XIIe siècle," Annales: économies, sociétés, civilisations, 39(1984), 454-79.

Concentrates on the decades immediately following dynastic union with Aragon in 1137 and the formation of the cultural and political identity of Catalonia, particularly under the rule of Raymond Berengar IV (1131-1162).

325. Bisson, Thomas N., "Mediterranean Territorial Power in the Twelfth Century," Proceedings of the American Philosophical Society, 123(1979), 143-50.
Though affected by many of the same stimuli as their northern counterparts, territorial governments in the Elbo valley and central Italy experienced a relatively high degree of continuity in public territorial order. This continuity in turn inhibited the development of a feudal structure similar to that found in the north.

326. Bouchard, Constance B., Spirituality and Administration: The Role of the Bishop in Twelfth-Century Auxerre (Cambridge, MA: Mediaeval Academy of America, 1979).
The lives of seven bishops of Auxerre, written in the twelfth and early thirteenth centuries, are analyzed in this study. Concludes that an early-twelfth-century fascination for the spiritual attributes of a bishop gave way by the end of the period to a standard of administrative ability by which the subjects were chiefly judged.

327. Duby, Georges, La société aux XIe et XIIe siècles dans la région Mâconnaise (Paris: A. Colin, 1953).
Integrates the methods of political, social, and economic history in this study of lay society in Mâcon, a founding work in the Duby school of mentalité that remains a model for regional studies. See also his "Lignage, noblesse et chevalerie au XIIe siècle dans la région mâconnaise: une révision," Annales: économies, sociétés, civilisations, 27(1972), 803-23.

328. Fletcher, R., The Episcopate in the Kingdom of Léon in the Twelfth Century (Oxford: Oxford University Press, 1978).
Establishes a chronology for Leonese bishops, analyzes the episcopal acta on which this study is based, then

discusses the nature of Leonese church government and its relation to the papacy. Bibliography included.

329. Freedman, Paul H., The Diocese of Vic: Tradition and Regeneration in Medieval Catalonia (New Brunswick: Rutgers University Press, 1983).
Recounts the rise and fall of a Catalan cathedral community. Using legal and political approaches to institutions and power, follows the diocese through periods of preeminence in the tenth and eleventh centuries and decline in the twelfth century.

330. Koziol, Geoffrey, "Law, Lordship, and Ritual: Political Order in the Diocese of Noyon (1000-1150)." Ph.D. dissertation: Stanford University, 1982.
The limited visibility of formal legal institutions in early Capetian France should not be interpreted as feudal anarchy. Rather, two informal methods of conflict resolution--conciliary trials and personal petitions--provided an orderly means of obtaining justice.

331. Mundy, John H., Liberty and Political Power in Toulouse, 1050-1230 (New York: Columbia University Press, 1954).
Toulouse was unusually independent and powerful for a twelfth-century city. Mundy accounts for this with a social history of the city's constitution, moving from physical and institutional descriptions to the evolution of political power, the transfer of power from count to count, and the means used to exercise power.

332. Painter, Sidney, "The Lords of Lusignan in the Eleventh and Twelfth Centuries," Speculum, 32(1957), 27-47.
Chronicles the evolution of a tenth-century landed family into a major presence in thirteenth-century Poitou and a baronial power of international importance. Reprinted in F.A. Cazel, ed., Feudalism and Liberty: Articles and Addresses of Sidney Painter (Baltimore: Johns Hopkins University Press, 1961), 41-72, which contains several other accounts of families and houses during the central Middle Ages.

333. Shideler, John, <u>A Medieval Catalan Noble Family: The Montcadas, 1000-1230</u> (Berkeley: University of California Press, 1983).
>Recounts the rise of a noble Catalan family during the central Middle Ages, relating their fortunes to major social and economic trends of the period.

334. Strait, Paul, <u>Cologne in the Twelfth Century</u> (Gainesville: University Presses of Florida, 1974).
>Political alignments and urban institutions in Cologne underwent considerable change during the twelfth century. While not revolutionary, changes in Cologne were dramatic, particularly the formation of an urban community and the emergence of administrative institutions that began to replace lordship as a means of government.

335. Urry, William, <u>Canterbury under the Angevin Kings</u>, 2 vols. (London: Athlone Press, 1967).
>Details the structure and development of government, the nature and interests of various groups of residents, and the changing topography of the borough. Volume one consists of a narrative and texts; volume two contains maps for the years 1166 and 1200.

336. Wightman, Wilfred E., <u>The Lacy Family in England and Normandy, 1066-1194</u> (Oxford: Clarendon Press, 1966).
>This history of the Hereford and Yorkshire Lacys through the twelfth century provides an opportunity to study the absorption of some large Anglo-Saxon holdings by the Anglo-Norman manorial system.

3.2 Additional Works

337. Barthélemy, Dominique, <u>Les deux ages de la seigneurie banale: pouvoir et société dans la terre des sires de Coucy (milieu XIe-milieu XIIIe s.)</u> (Paris: Publications de la Sorbonne, 1984).
338. Chedeville, Andre, <u>Chartres et ses campagnes, XIe-XIIIe siècles</u> (Paris, Klincksieck, 1973).

339. Crouch, David, The Beaumont Twins: The Roots and Branches of Power in the Twelfth Century (Cambridge, England: Cambridge University Press, 1986).
340. Décarreaux, Jean, Normands, papes et moines: cinquante ans de conquêtes et de politique religieuse en Italie méridionale et en Sicile (milieu du XIe siècle-début du XIIe) (Paris: A. & J. Picard, 1974).
341. English, Barbara, The Lords of Holderness, 1086-1260: A Study in Feudal Society (Oxford: Oxford University Press, 1979).
342. Freed, John B., The Counts of Falkanstein: Noble Self-Consciousness in Twelfth-Century Germany, Transactions of the American Philosophical Society, 74:6 (Philadelphia: American Philosophical Society, 1984).
343. Galasso, Giuseppe, "Social and Political Developments in the Eleventh and Twelfth Centuries," in The Normans in Sicily and Southern Italy (Oxford: Oxford University Press, 1977), 47-63.
344. Hollister, C. Warren, "The Misfortunes of the Mandevilles," Monarchy, Magnates and Institutions in the Anglo-Norman World (London: Hambledon Press, 1986), 117-127. Originally published in History, 58(1973), 18-28.
345. Hyde, John K., Society and Politics in Medieval Italy: The Evolution of the Civil Life, 1000-1350 (London, Macmillan, 1973).
346. Krautheimer, Richard, Rome: Profile of a City, 312-1308 (Princeton: Princeton University Press, 1980).
347. Kupper, Jean L., Liège et l'église impériale, XIe-XIIe siècles (Paris: Belles lettres, 1981).
348. Lane, Frederic C., Venice, a Maritime Republic (Baltimore: Johns Hopkins University Press, 1973).
349. Lewis, Archibald R., "The Guillems of Montpellier: A Sociological Appraisal," Viator, 2(1971), 159-69.
350. Locatelli, René and R. Fiétier, "Naissance et essor du comté de Bourgogne (XIe-XIIIe siècles)," in R. Fiétier, Histoire de la Franche-Comté (Toulouse: J. Privat, 1977), 121-61.
351. Loud, G. A., Church and Society in the Norman Principality of Capua, 1058-1197 (Oxford: Clarendon Press, 1985).
352. Meisel, Janet, Barons of the Welsh Frontier: The Corbet, Pantulf and Fitz-Warin Families, 1066-1272 (Lincoln: University of Nebraska Press, 1980).

353. Mundy, John H., "Urban Society and Culture: Toulouse and its Region," in R. Benson and G. Constable, eds., <u>Renaissance and Renewal in the Twelfth Century</u> (Cambridge, MA: Harvard University Press, 1982), 229-47.
354. Musset, Lucien, "Gouvernés et gouvernants dans la monde scandinave et dans le monde normand (XIe-XIIe siècles)," <u>Recueils de la Société Jean Bodin pour l'histoire comparative des institutions</u>, 23(1970), 439-68.
355. Nelson, Lynn H., <u>The Normans in South Wales, 1070-1171</u> (Austin: University of Texas Press, 1966)
356. Norwich, John J., <u>The Kingdom in the Sun, 1130-1194</u> (New York: Harper & Row, 1970).
357. Ourliac, Paul, "Realité au imaginaire: la féodalité toulousaine," in <u>Religion, société et politique: mélanges en hommage à Jacques Ellul</u> (Paris: Presses universitaires de France, 1983), 331-44.
358. Poly, Jean P., <u>La Provence et la société féodale, 879-1166</u> (Paris: Bordas, 1976).
359. Reynolds, Susan, <u>Kingdoms and Communities in Western Europe, 900-1300</u> (New York, 1984).
360. ------, "The Rulers of London in the 12th Century," <u>History</u>, 57(1972), 337-53.
361. Rowland, Robert J., "The Decline of the Aristocracy in Eleventh and Twelfth Century Sardinia," <u>Quaderni Italianistica</u>, 4(1983), 198-207.
362. Schmugge, Ludwig, "Ministerialität und Bürgertum im Reims: Untersuchungen zur Geschichte der Stadt im 12. und 13. Jahrhundert," <u>Francia</u>, 2(1974), 152-212.
363. Waley, Daniel P., <u>The Italian City-Republics</u> (New York: McGraw-Hill, 1969).

3.2 Related Entries

<u>Section 2.1.1</u>: 43, 49, 51, 57, 58, 60, 71, 72, 89, 94, 98; <u>section 2.1.2</u>: 106; <u>section 3.1</u>: 245; <u>section 3.3</u>: 405

3.3 Law, Administration, Taxation, and Institutions

364. Avril, Jospeh, Le gouvernement des évêques et la vie religieuse dans la diocèse d'Angers (1148-1240) (Lille: Université de Lille III, 1984?).

Principally an administrative history of the Diocese of Angers during this period, particularly the implementation of administrative reform during a time of considerable change. Preliminary chapters provide a general social, political, and economic survey of the region.

365. Baldwin, John W., The Government of Philip Augustus: Foundations of French Royal Power in the Middle Ages (Berkeley: University of California Press, 1986).

A thorough account of the revolution in the French monarchy and government effected by Philip Augustus (1165-1223). Argues that the turning point occurred with arrangements for governance made when Philip departed for the Third Crusade, rather than (as conventionally held) following the conquest of Normandy and Anjou.

366. Bautier, Robert H., ed., La France de Philippe Auguste; le temps de mutation: actes du Colloque international, Paris, 1980 (Paris: Centre national de la recherche scientifique, 1982).

Fifty papers presented at a 1980 conference include a section on "Les moyens du gouvernement" with ten papers divided into the subsections, "La chancellerie," "Les aspects juridiques," "Comptabilité et monnaie," and "L'armée et la marine."

367. Berman, Harold J., Law and Revolution: The Formation of the Western Legal Tradition (Cambridge, MA: Harvard University Press, 1983).

Massive study of the formation of European legal institutions, principles, and concepts, focusing on the eleventh through thirteenth centuries. Part one deals with the papal revolution and part two concerns secular legal systems. A work both of interpretation and of reference.

368. Bisson, Thomas N., "The Organized Peace in Southern France and Catalonia, ca. 1140-ca. 1233," American Historical Review, 82(1977), 290-311.

Argues that the Peace of God provided the principal coercive structure for the maintenance of public order. This structure, which survived the Albigensian crusades, perhaps accounts for the failure of feudal relations to develop according to the northern European model.

369. Bournazel, Eric, Le gouvernement capétien au XIIe siècle, 1108-1180 (Paris: Presses universitaires de France, 1975).

Extends J. Lemarignier's Le gouvernement royal aux premiers temps Capétiens, 987-1108 (Paris: A. & J. Picard, 1965) and concentrates on the persons and evolving structures closest to the French monarchs of the twelfth century. Chiefly concerned with the shift from the largely private to the largely public activities of royal associates on behalf of the king as the members of the king's familia became the king's consiliarii.

370. Caenegem, Raoul C. van, The Birth of the English Common Law (Cambridge, England: Cambridge University Press, 1973).

A collection of four lectures delivered at Cambridge University in 1968: "English Courts from the Conqueror to Glanville," "Royal Writs and Writ Procedure," "The Jury in the Royal Courts," and "English Law and the Continent." The final lecture argues that England failed to follow the continent in adopting a legal system based on Roman law because uniquely English practices took root well before mature alternatives to Roman law became available.

371. ------, "The Law of Evidence in the Twelfth Century," in S. Kuttner and J. Ryan, eds., Proceedings of the Second International Congress of Medieval Canon Law, Boston College, 1963 (Vatican City: S. Congregatio de seminariis et studiorum universitatibus, 1965), 297-310.

A "primitive" evidentiary system typified by ordeals and compurgation began in the twelfth century to give way to a "rational" system based on witnesses and written documents. Such changes were but one expression of a broader psychological change in attitude toward law, government, and other institutions.

372. Caenegem, Raoul C. van, "Public Prosecution of Crime in Twelfth-Century England," in C. Brooke et al., eds., Church and Government in the Middle Ages: Essays Presented to C.R. Cheney on His 70th Birthday (Cambridge, England: Cambridge University Press, 1976), 41-76.

Analyzes twelfth-century English experiments in criminal prosecution and the emergence of the jury of presentment during the reign of Henry II (1133-1189), particularly with the assizes of Clarendon (1166) and Northampton (1176).

373. Campbell, James, "The Significance of the Anglo-Norman State in the Administrative History of Western Europe," in W. Paravicini and K. Werner, eds., Histoire comparée de l'administration (IVe-XVIIIe siècles): actes du XIVe Colloque historique franco-allemand, Tours, 1977 (Munich: Artemis Press, 1980), 117-34.

Several important administrative techniques were developed and diffused by the Anglo-Norman state. Even more important was an increased use of written records for the administration of estates and a great proliferation of written documents as the basis for transacting business and participating in the legal system.

374. Constable, Giles, "Cluniac Administration and Administrators in the Twelfth Century," Cluniac Studies (London: Variorum Reprints, 1980), essay two.

The generalization of a highly centralized network of Cluniac monasteries personally controlled by a single abbot is not valid for the late eleventh and twelfth centuries. While Peter the Venerable (1092-1156) to some extent used the traditional administrative techniques of visitation and written communication, he found chapter-general meetings, frequent transfer of priors, and recruitment of good administrators to be more effective techniques. Originally published in W.C. Jordan et al., eds., Order and Innovation in the Middle Ages: Essays in Honor of Jospeh R. Strayer (Princeton: Princeton University Press, 1976), 17-30, 417-24.

375. Green, Judith A., The Government of England under Henry I (Cambridge, England: Cambridge University Press, 1986).
   An administrative history of England during Henry I's (1068-1135) reign and a prosopographical study of 104 participants in Henry's government in 1130. Explores such issues as the development of a central administration distinct from the royal household and the evolution of the office of justiciar, and investigates the social origins of Henry's "new men."

376. Hehl, Ernst D., Kirche und Krieg im 12. Jahrhundert: Studien zur kanonischem Recht und politischer Wirklichkeit (Stuttgart: A. Hiersemann, 1980).
   Draws on the work of Gratian (d. c. 1179) and other decretists to assess the Church's attitudes toward warfare in the late twelfth century. Serves as an extension of item 421 in section 3.4 and includes a lengthy bibliography.

377. Hollister, C. Warren and J. Baldwin, "The Rise of Administrative Kingship: Henry I and Philip Augustus," Monarchy, Magnates and Institutions in the Anglo-Norman World (London: Hambledon Press, 1986), 223-45.
   Compares the contributions of two kings critical in the development of the administrative institutions of their respective kingdoms. Hollister points to the appearance of the exchequer, the use of justices in eyre, and the concentration of authority in the hands of Roger of Salisbury (d. 1139) as evidence of Henry I's (1068-1135) policy of centralization. Baldwin emphasizes the introduction of fixed archives, a financial court of audit, traveling justices, and a viceregency as examples of a similar policy in Philip Augustus (1165-1223). Originally published in American Historical Review, 83(1978), 867-905.

378. Hyams, Paul R., Kings, Lords and Peasants in Medieval England: The Common Law of Villeinage in the Twelfth and Thirteenth Centuries (Oxford: Oxford University Press, 1980).
   Analyzes the structure and concept of villeinage from a legal perspective by comparing plea roll cases and contemporary legal theory beginning in the late twelfth

century. Finds considerable discrepancy between practice and theory, concluding that "serfdom" defines social and economic conditions but "servile villeinage" more aptly describes the legal status of this stratum. Includes sizable bibliography. Also see P. Vinogradoff, Villainage in England: Essays in English Mediaeval History (Oxford: Clarendon Press, 1892).

379. Kealey, Edward J., Roger of Salisbury, Viceroy of England (Berkeley: University of California Press, 1972).
Twelfth-century prelates who achieved high secular office make fascinating subjects for biographical studies. Kealey takes full advantage of his opportunity, using this subject as an avenue into parallel examinations of royal and ecclesiastical institutions.

380. Kuttner, Stephan G., Harmony from Dissonance: An Interpretation of Medieval Canon Law (Latrope, PA: Archabbey Press, 1960).
The classic interpretation of Gratian (d. c. 1179) and his impact on canon law. Frequently used to characterize the essence of the twelfth-century renaissance. Delivered as a lecture in 1956.

381. ------, "The Revival of Jurisprudence," in R. Benson and G. Constable, eds., Renaissance and Renewal in the Twelfth Century (Cambridge, MA: Harvard University Press, 1982), 299-323.
Discusses the reappearance of Justinian's Digest, the general intellectual background of the twelfth century, and the historiography of medieval law since C.H. Haskins, then surveys the methods, forms, centers, and masters of the "new jurisprudence."

382. Nörr, Knut W., "Institutional Foundations of the New Jurisprudence," in R. Benson and G. Constable, eds., Renaissance and Renewal in the Twelfth Century (Cambridge, MA: Harvard University Press, 1982), 324-38.
Describes the educational, secular, and ecclesiastical institutions associated with twelfth-century jurisprudence. Accompanied by a substantial bibliography.

383. Richardson, Henry G. and G. Sayles, The Governance of Mediaeval England from the Conquest to Magna Carta (Edinburgh: Edinburgh University Press, 1963).
   Some portions have been replaced by more recent works but this title remains the leading interpretation of twelfth-century English government. Also see the authors' companion study, Law and Legislation from Aethelberht to Magna Carta (Edinburgh: Edinburgh University Press, 1966).

384. Stenton, Doris M., English Justice Between the Norman Conquest and the Great Charter, 1066-1215 (Philadelphia: American Philosophical Society, 1964).
   Three lectures from 1961 and another delivered in 1958, plus six critical notes. The first lecture ("The Anglo-Saxon Inheritance") provides an overview of Anglo-Saxon conceptions of law while the remaining lectures ("The Angevin Leap Forward," "Courts of Justice and the Beginning of the Legal Profession," and "King John and the Courts of Justice") consider aspects of the Angevin legal system.

385. Turner, Ralph V., "Roman Law in England Before the Time of Bracton," Journal of British Studies, 15(1975-76), 1-25.
   Discusses early authors and works influenced by Roman law, English scholars who studied or otherwise promoted Roman law at home or abroad, the development of Roman legal studies in England, and the negligible impact of Roman law on common law.

3.3 Aditional Works

386. Baldwin, John W., "Critics of the Legal Profession: Peter the Chanter and His Circle," in S. Kuttner and J. Ryan, eds., Proceedings of the Second International Congress of Medieval Canon Law, Boston College, 1963 (Vatican City: S. Congregatio de seminariis et studiorum universitatibus, 1965), 249-59.

387. Bosl, Karl, Die Reichsministerialität der Salier und Staufer: ein Beitrag zur Geschichte des hochmittelalterlichen deutschen Volkes, Staates und Reiches (Stuttgart: A. Hiersemann, 1950-51).

388. Caenegem, Raoul C. van, Royal Writs in England from the Conquest to Glanvill (London: B. Quaritch, 1959).
389. Cheney, Christopher R., From Becket to Langton: English Church Government, 1170-1213 (Manchester: Manchester University Press, 1956).
390. Duggan, Charles, "The Reception of Canon Law in England in the Later Twelfth Century," Canon Law in Medieval England: The Becket Dispute and Decretal Collections (London: Variorum Reprints, 1982), essay 11.
391. ------, Twelfth-Century Decretal Collections and Their Importance in English History (London: University of London, 1963).
392. Genicot, Léopold, "Problèmes et méthodes de gouvernement au XIIe siècle," Reuve d'histoire ecclésiastique, 72(1977), 326-32.
393. Gillingham, John and J. C. Holt, eds., War and Government in the Middle Ages: Essays in Honour of J.O. Prestwich (Cambridge, England: Boydell Press, 1984).
394. Hamilton, Bernard, The Latin Church in the Crusader States: The Secular Church (London: Variorum Publications, 1980).
395. Harvey, Sally P., "Domesday Book and Anglo-Norman Governance," Transactions of the Royal Historical Society, 5th ser., 25(1975), 175-93.
396. Herkenrath, Rainer M., Die Reichskanzlei in den Jahren 1174 bis 1180 (Vienna: Österreichische Akademie der Wissenschaften, 1977).
397. ------, Die Reichskanzlei in den Jahren 1181 bis 1190 (Vienna: Österreichische Akademie der Wissenschaften, 1985).
398. Hollister, C. Warren, "The Origins of the English Treasury," Monarchs, Magnates and Institutions in the Anglo-Norman World (London: Hambledon Press, 1986), 209-22. Originally published in English Historical Review, 93(1978), 262-75.
399. Keefe, Thomas K., Feudal Assessments and the Political Community under Henry II and His Sons (Berkeley: University of California Press, 1983).
400. Kroeschell, Karl, "Recht und Rechtsbegriff im 12. Jahrhundert," in Probleme des 12. Jahrhunderts, Vorträge und Forschungen, 12 (Stuttgart: J. Thorbecke, 1968), 309-35.

401. Kupper, Jean L., "Bibliographie: la chancellerie impériale dans la seconde moitié du XIIe siècle," Moyen Age, 90(1984), 487-502.
402. Milsom, S. F., Historical Foundations of the Common Law, 2d ed. (Toronto: Butterworths, 1981).
403. ------, The Legal Framework of English Feudalism: The Maitland Lectures Given in 1972 (Cambridge, England: Cambridge University Press, 1976).
404. ------, "Inheritance by Women in the Twelfth and Early Thirteenth Centuries," in M. Arnold et al., eds., On the Laws and Customs of England: Essays of Samuel E. Thorne (Chapel Hill: University of North Carolina Press, 1981), 60-89.
405. Palmer, Robert C., The County Courts of Medieval England, 1150-1350 (Princeton: Princeton University Press, 1982).
406. Post, Gaines, Studies in Medieval Legal Thought: Public Law and the State, 1100-1322 (Princeton: Princeton University Press, 1964).
407. Rathbone, Eleanor, "Roman Law in the Anglo-Norman Realm," Studia gratiana, 11(1967), 253-71.
408. Sass, Stephen L., "Medieval Roman Law: A Guide to the Sources and Literature," Law Library Journal, 58(1965), 130-59.
409. Sutherland, Donald W., The Assize of Novel Disseisin (Oxford: Clarendon Press, 1973).
410. Takayama, Hiróshi, "The Financial and Administrative Organization of the Norman Kingdom of Sicily," Viator, 16(1985), 129-57.
411. Turner, Ralph V., The English Judiciary in the Age of Glanvill and Bracton, c. 1176-1239 (Cambridge, England: Cambridge University Press, 1985).
412. ------, "Twelfth- and Thirteenth-Century English Law and Government: Suggestions for Prosopographical Approaches," Medieval Prosopography, 3(1982), 21-34.
413. Warren, W.L., "The Myth of Norman Administrative Efficiency," Transactions of the Royal Historical Society, 5th ser., 34(1984), 113-32.
414. West, Francis J., The Justiciarship in England, 1066-1232 (Cambridge, England: Cambridge University Press, 1966).

3.3 Related Items

Section 2.1.1: 101; section 2.2: 139; section 3.1: 218, 225, 250, 265, 272, 296, 307, 317, 321; section 3.2: 326, 330, 331, 362; section 3.4: 418; section 4.2: 491; section 4.3.2: 591; section 4.4.3: 721.

3.4 Armed Conflict

415. Atiya, Aziz S., Crusade, Commerce and Culture (Bloomington: Indiana University Press, 1962.
   Sets a context for an analysis of central medieval crusades by distinguishing between the crusade, a continuing movement with an origin well before the Middle Ages, and the crusades, a series of military expeditions beginning in the central Middle Ages. This distinction is then associated with the "Eastern question," itself a concept that begins well before and continues well after the eleventh and twelfth centuries.

416. ------, The Crusade: Historiography and Bibliography (Bloomington: Indiana University Press, 1962).
   A companion volume to the author's Crusade, Commerce and Culture, item 415. Several hundred entries for both primary and secondary works are preceded by a brief historiographical essay that focuses on interpretations prior to the twentieth century.

417. Beeler, John, Warfare in England, 1066-1189 (Ithaca: Cornell University Press, 1966).
   Recounts the military history of England in the twelfth century, beginning with Hastings (1066) and concluding with engagements on the marches of Wales (to the death of Henry II in 1189). Narrations of battles, including their circumstances, tactics, and military consequences, are supplemented with two chapters on military organization and a substantial bibliography. See also Beeler's Warfare in Feudal Europe, 730-1200 (Ithaca: Cornell University Press, 1971).

418. Brundage, James A., <u>Medieval Canon Law and the Crusader</u> (Madison: University of Wisconsin Press, 1969).
   Studies the ecclesiastical theory of crusade as embodied in the crusader's vow, concentrating on the decretalists' regard for the vow, obligations of crusaders, and the spiritual and temporal privileges of the Cross. Accompanied by a select yet extensive bibliography.

419. Cahen, Claude, <u>Orient et occident au temps des croisades</u> (Paris: Aubier Montaigne, 1983).
   Provides useful background material relating to the social, intellectual, and economic conditions preceding and during the crusades. Footnotes are extensive and the select bibliography, while short, is useful.

420. Cowdrey, H. E., "Pope Urban II's Preaching of the First Crusade," <u>History</u>, 55(1970), 177-88.
   Surveys the sources for Urban II's (pope, 1088-1099) call to crusade--chronicles, charters, letters, polemical literature, and Urban's own writings--and concludes that the pope intended the crusade to seek the liberation of Jerusalem. Contains a review of the Erdmann thesis and its challengers. Valuable primarily for its discussions of primary and secondary sources.

421. Erdmann, Carl, <u>Die Entstehung des Kreuzzugsgedankens</u> (Stuttgart: W. Kohlhammer, 1935). Translated by M. Baldwin and W. Goffart as <u>The Origin of the Idea of Crusade</u> (Princeton: Princeton University Press, 1977).
   Traces the evolution of various elements that combined to form the idea of crusade--largely the militarization of a Church that a millennium earlier had been founded on pacifism, but also the development of a popular crusade idea and the opportunism of Urban II (pope, 1088-1099). See related item 376 in section 3.3.

422. Hollister, C. Warren, <u>The Military Organization of Norman England</u> (Oxford: Clarendon Press, 1965).
   Analyzes the introduction and nature of Norman feudalism and the surviving elements of Anglo-Saxon military service.

Maintains that initially Norman military organization was radically different from its predecessor in England. The Anglo-Saxons, however, greatly influenced Norman methods and so contributed substantially to the development of Anglo-Norman military organization.

423. Lilie, Ralph J., Byzanz und die Kreuzfahrerstaaten: Studien zur Politik des Byzantinischen Reiches gegenüber den Staaten der Kreuzfahrer in Syrien und Palästina bis zum vierten Kreuzzug (1096-1204) (Munich: W. Fink, 1981).

Studies the relations between Byzantium and the Crusader States in the context of those between Byzantium and the Latin West, particularly during the reigns of Alexius I (1098-1118), John II (1118-1143), and Manuel I (1143-1180). Extensive notes and bibliography.

424. Mayer, Hans E., Geschichte der Kreuzzüge (Stuttgart: W. Kohlhammer, 1965). Translated by J. Gillingham as The Crusades, 2d ed. (Oxford: Oxford University Press, 1988).

Generally regarded as the leading narrative survey of the crusades.

425. ------, Bibliographie zur Geschichte der Kreuzzüge (Hannover: Hansche Buchhandlung, 1960).

Covers over 5,300 titles and offers the special advantage of access to non-English works. Updated with his "Literaturbericht über die Geschichte der Kreuzzüge: Veröffentlichungen, 1958-1967," Historische Zeitschrift, Sonderheft, 3 (Munich, 1969).

426. Morris, Colin, "Propaganda for War: The Dissemination of the Crusading Ideal in the Twelfth Century," Studies in Church History, 20(1983), 79-101.

Examines the dynamics and content of such crusading propaganda as public appeals, rumors, sermons, recruiting songs. Concludes that "crusading propaganda was one aspect of the new social forms and means of communication which were characteristic of the period" (p. 100).

427. Riley-Smith, Jonathan, "The Crusades," History Today, 32:4(April 1982), 48-49.

A very good bibliographic survey of the leading works in many areas of crusade historiography and a point of departure for anyone unfamiliar with the literature.

428. Riley-Smith, Jonathan, The First Crusade and the Idea of Crusading (London: Athlone Press, 1986).
Views the first crusade as the ideological embodiment of the late-eleventh-century spiritual reform movement. Robert the Monk (12th century), Guibert of Nogent (1064?-c. 1125), and Baldric of Bourgueil (1046-1130) later provided the legitimating theological refinements.

429. Runciman, Steven, A History of the Crusades, 3 vols. (Cambridge, England: Cambridge University Press, 1951-54).
Though now somewhat dated, this opus magnum remains the leading English-language survey. Also useful for a general orientation is the collection of articles by specialists in K. Setton, ed., A History of the Crusades, 2d ed., 6 vols. (Madison, 1969-). Volume 1 of the Setton collection is The First Hundred Years, 2d ed. (Madison: University of Wisconsin Press, 1969).

430. Siberry, Elizabeth, Criticism of Crusading: 1095-1274 (Oxford: Clarendon Press, 1985).
Counters the prevailing view that the crusades declined in popularity as the thirteenth century wore on. Instead argues that what previously were regarded as criticisms of the crusades were in fact criticisms of abuses and the crusades' promoters. Concludes that genuine criticism of crusades per se was rare. Very good bibliography of both primary and secondary works.

431. Smail, R. C., Crusading Warfare (1097-1193) (Cambridge, England: Cambridge University Press, 1956).
Analyzes the military resources (both human and material), organization, weapons, embattlements, and tactics of both Latins and Arabs relevant to the Latin enclaves in Syria.

3.3 Additional Works

432. Alphandéry, Paul, Chrétienté et l'idée de croisade, 2 vols. (Paris: A. Michel, 1954), vol 1: Les premières croisades.
433. Bartlett, Robert J., "Technique militaire et pouvoir politique, 900-1300," Annales: économies, sociétés, civilisations, 41(1986), 1135-59.
434. Blake, Ernest O., "The Formation of the 'Crusade Idea,'" Journal of Ecclesiastical History, 21(1970), 11-31.
435. ------, "A Hermit Goes to War: Peter and the Origins of the First Crusade," Studies in Church History, 22(1985), 79-107.
436. Boehm, L., "Gesta Dei per Francos--oder Gesta Francorum? Die Kreuzzüge als Historiographisches Problem," Saeculum, 8(1957), 43-81.
437. Brundage, James A., ed., The Crusades: Motives and Achievements (Boston: D.C. Heath, 1964).
438. ------, "Recent Crusade Historiography: Some Observations and Suggestions," Catholic Historical Review, 49(1963-64), 493-507.
439. Christiansen, Eric, The Northern Crusades: The Baltic and the Catholic Frontier, 1100-1525 (Minneapolis: University of Minnesota Press, 1980).
440. Contamine, Philippe, War in the Middle Ages (New York: B. Blackwell, 1984).
441. Cowdrey, H. E., "Cluny and the First Crusade," Revue bénédictine, 83(1973), 285-311.
442. Delaruelle, Etienne, L'idée de croisade au moyen age (Turin: Bottega d'Erasmo, 1980).
443. Forey, A. J., "Novitiate and Instruction in the Military Orders during the Twelfth and Thirteenth Centuries," Speculum, 61(1986), 1-17.
444. ------, "The Emergence of the Military Order in the Twelfth Century," Journal of Ecclesiastical History, 36(1985), 175-95.
445. ------, "The Military Orders and the Spanish Reconquest in the Twelfth and Thirteenth Centuries," Traditio, 40(1984), 197-234.
446. Geary, Patrick J., "Vivre en conflit dans une France sans état: typologie des mecanismes de règlement des conflits

(1050-1200)," Annales: économies, sociétés, civilisations, 41(1986), 1107-33.
447. Grabois, Aryeh, "De la trêve de Dieu à la paix du roi: étude sur les transformations du mouvement de la paix au XIIe siècle," in P. Gallais and Y. Riou, eds., Mélanges offerts à René Crozet, 2 vols. (Poitiers: Société d'études médiévales, 1966), 1:585-96.
448. Holdsworth, Christopher J., "Ideas and Reality: Some Attempts to Control and Defuse War in the Twelfth Century," Studies in Church History, 20(1983), 59-78.
449. Holt, P. M., ed., The Eastern Mediterranean Lands in the Period of the Crusades (Warminster, England: Aris and Phillips, 1977).
450. Prawer, Joshua, The Crusaders' Kingdom: European Colonialism in the Middle Ages (New York: Praeger, 1972).
451. ------, Histoire du Royaume Latin de Jérusalem, translated from Hebrew by G. Nahan, 2 vols. (Paris: Centre national de la recherche scientifique, 1969-70).
452. Riley-Smith, Jonathan, "The First Crusade and the Persecution of the Jews," Studies in Church History, 21(1984), 51-72.
453. Rousset, Paul, Les origines et les caractères de la première croisade (Geneva: A. Kundig, 1945).
454. Siberry, Elizabeth, "Missionaries and Crusaders, 1095-1274: Opponents or Allies?" Studies in Church History, 20(1983), 103-10.
455. Swan, Emmanuel, L'Islam et la croisade: idéologie et propagande dans les réactions musulmanes aux croisades (Paris: Librarie d'Amerique et d'Orient, 1968).

3.4 Related Entries

Section 2.1.2: 130; section 2.2: 144; section 3.1: 239, 249; section 3.3: 368, 376, 393, 394; section 4.2: 532; section 4.3.3: 614; section 4.5: 798.

4.0 CULTURE

4.1 Religious Experience and Spirituality

456. Bynum, Caroline Walker, "Docere verbo et exemplo": An Aspect of Twelfth-Century Spirituality (Missoula: Scholars Press, 1978).
   Uses the theme, "teaching by word and example," to illustrate the spiritual differences between regular canons and the new monastic orders. While both religious groups were socially aware and interested in service to others, regular canons were more likely to seek the edification of others through speech and behavior. A substantial bibliography supplements the work.

457. Chatillon, Jean, "The Spiritual Renaissance of the End of the Eleventh and the Beginning of the Twelfth Century," American Benedictine Review, 36(1985), 292-317.
   Reviews and summarizes the religious and spiritual revolution of an "often obscure army of monks, religious, hermits, preachers, clerics and laymen which was then on the march" (p. 292).

458. Constable, Giles, "Twelfth-Century Spirituality and the Late Middle Ages," Medieval and Renaissance Studies, 5(1971 for 1969), 27-60.
   Looks to the late eleventh and twelfth centuries for developments in medieval spirituality that shaped the religious backdrop for the Renaissance. Focuses on the emergence of

an inward-looking and affective piety, criticism of monasticism as an institution, and popular religious interest in devotions and liturgy.

459. Constable, Giles, "The Diversity of Religious Life and Acceptance of Social Pluralism in the Twelfth Century," in D. Beales and G. Best, eds., History, Society and the Churches: Essays in Honour of Owen Chadwick (Cambridge, England: Cambridge University Press, 1985), 29-47.

Assesses the dynamics and implications of the movement from a unity to a multiplicity of forms of religious life. Concludes the twelfth century witnessed great change in social and religious values, eventually accepted these changes, but did not regard all new forms of religious life as equally valuable.

460. Leclercq, Jean, Nouveau visage de Bernard de Clairvaux: approches psycho-historiques (Paris: Cerf, 1976).

As much a study of the psychology of sainthood in general as of Bernard's (1090-1153) sainthood. Vignettes look at an early life of Bernard, Bernard as psychotherapist, Bernard and the feminine, psychology and saintliness, and other topics related to twelfth-century spirituality. Also see related item 495 in section 4.2 for similar psycho-historical studies on monasticism.

461. Little, Lester K., Religious Poverty and the Profit Economy in Medieval Europe (Ithaca: Cornell University Press, 1978).

Examines the spiritual crisis of urban religious life during M. Bloch's second feudal age, the eleventh through thirteenth centuries. The crucial element in this crisis was the influence voluntary poverty and scholastic social thought had on the formation of new, distinctly urban attitudes toward wealth and poverty.

462. McDonnell, Ernest W., "The vita apostolica: Diversity or Dissent?" Church History, 24(1955), 15-31.

Articulates the basic principles of the vita apostolica and surveys uses of the concept for both reform and dissent. Examples range from the Gregorian Reform of the late eleventh century through the thirteenth century.

463. McGinn, Bernard and J. Meyendorff, eds., <u>Christian Spirituality: Origins to the Twelfth Century</u> (New York: Crossroads Publishing, 1985).

The section, "Religious World of the Twelfth Century," consists of a brief bibliographic survey by McGinn; B. Ward, "Anselm of Canterbury and His Influence"; M. Pennington, "The Cistercians"; and G. Zinn, "The Regular Canons." Articles include bibliographies of sources and modern works.

464. Morris, Colin, "Individualism in Twelfth-Century Religion: Some Further Reflections," <u>Journal of Ecclesiastical History</u>, 31(1980), 195-206.

Affirms the greater part of item 5 (section 1.1), offers modifications of some points made in that article, and provides additional comments. Modifications center on the nature of religious communities, the relationship of an individual to such a group, and changes in the structure and character of the Church. Also draws a distinction between discovery of the individual and discovery of the self.

465. Trout, John M. "Preaching by the Laity in the Twelfth Century," <u>Studies in Medieval Culture</u>, 4(1973-74), 92-108.

Lay persons during the twelfth century often preached and many were condemned for heresy. Concludes that although lay preaching was strongly disapproved, it was not categorically proscribed and some lay persons even were encouraged by ecclesiastics to preach.

466. Ward, Benedicta, <u>Miracles and the Medieval Mind: Theory, Record and Event, 1000-1215</u>, rev. ed. (Philadelphia: University of Pennsylvania Press, 1982).

Examines the place of miracles in life and society, as well as the content, structure, and uses of miracle stories. Includes a lengthy bibliography of primary and secondary works.

4.1 Additional Works

467. Bethell, Denis, "The Making of a Twelfth-Century Relic Collection," Studies in Church History, 8(1972), 61-72.
468. Bolton, Brenda M., "Via ascetica: A Papal Quandry," Studies in Church History, 22(1985), 161-91.
469. Brooke, Christopher N., "Monk and Canon: Some Patterns in the Religious Life of the Twelfth Century," Studies in Church History, 22(1985), 109-29.
470. Bynum, Caroline Walker, "The Spirituality of Regular Canons in the Twelfth Century: A New Approach," Mediaevalia et humanistica, Ser. 2, 4(1973), 3-24.
471. Constable, Giles, Religious Life and Thought (11th-12th Centuries) (London: Variorum Reprints, 1979).
472. Evans, Gillian R., "A Change of Mind in Some Scholars in the Eleventh and Early Twelfth Century," Studies in Church History, 15(1978), 27-38.
473. Harper-Bill, C., "The Piety of the Anglo-Norman Knightly Class," in R.A. Brown, ed., Anglo-Norman Studies (Proceedings of the Battle Conference on Anglo-Norman Studies), 2(1980 for 1979), 63-77.
474. Javelet, Robert, "Psychologie des auteurs spirituels du XIIe siècle," Revue des sciences religieuses, 33(1959), 18-64, 97-164, 209-68.
475. Mayr-Harting, Henry, "Functions of a Twelfth-Century Recluse," History, 60(1975), 337-52.
476. ------, "Functions of a Twelfth-Century Shrine: The Miracles of St. Frideswide," in H. Mayr-Harting and R.I. Moore, eds., Studies in Medieval History Presented to R.H.C. Davis (London: Hambledon Press, 1985), 193-206.
477. Newman, Barbara, "Hildegard of Bingen: Visions and Validation," Church History, 54(1985), 163-75.
478. Pycke, Jacques, Le chapitre cathédral Notre-Dame de Tournai de la fin du XIe à la fin du XIIIe siècle: son organisation, sa vie, ses membres (Louvain: Nauwelaerts, 1986).
479. Rousset, Paul, "La notion de Chrétienté aux XIe et XIIe siècles," Moyen Age, 69(1963), 191-203.
480. Sigal, Pierre A., L'homme et le miracle dans la France médiévale, XIe-XIIe siècle (Paris: Cerf, 1985).

481. Spätling, Luchesius G., "Franz von Assisi und das ausgehende 12. Jahrhundert," Archivum franciscanum historicum, 75(1982), 72-88.

4.1 Related Entries

Section 1.1: 4; section 2.1.1: 55; section 2.2: 138, 143; section 2.3: in toto; section 4.2: 483, 485, 496; section 4.3.3: 614, 620; section 4.3.4: 630; section 4.4.3: 752, 755.

4.2 Monasticism and Monastic Culture

482. Brooke, Christopher N., The Monastic World, 1000-1300 (London: P. Elek, 1974).
    Appears to be just another coffeetable book with nice pictures and arid text. Nice pictures (contriubted by art historian Wim Swaan) are included but are supplemented by substantive text. A chapter on the twelfth century summarizes the important monastic contributions to this period in art and architecture, persons and institutions, and letters and humanism.

483. Bynum, Caroline Walker, "The Cistercian Conception of Community: An Aspect of Twelfth-Century Spirituality," Harvard Theological Review, 68(1975), 273-86.
    Twelfth-century Cistercians were concerned more than Benedictines with interpersonal relations and the concept of community. This difference caused a creative tension between traditional (Benedictine) notions of monasticism and the twelfth-century ideal of service to one's neighbor. Reprinted in her Jesus as Mother: Studies in the Spirituality of the High Middle Ages (Berkeley: University of California Press, 1984).

484. Cantor, Norman F., "The Crisis of Western Monasticism, 1050-1130," American Historical Review, 66(1960), 47-67.
    In the early Middle Ages, Benedictine monasticism was co-extensive with medieval civilization. At the turn of the eleventh and twelfth centuries, several factors

combined to remove intellectual, political, and educational leadership from monastic centers. Political developments, demographic and economic growth, and changing religious values all combined to disrupt "the early medieval equilibrium between the Church and the world."

485. Chatillon, Jean, "La crise de l'église aux XIe et XIIe siècles et les origines des grandes fédérations canoniales," Revue d'histoire de la spiritualité, 53(1977), 3-45.

Argues that the inception and proliferation of canonical orders occurred largely in response to an eleventh- and twelfth-century spiritual crisis within the Church. A growing desire for a religious lifestyle that emphasized evangelical poverty and communal living, yet was not in the institutional mainstream of the Church, provided the impetus for these federations.

486. Chibnall, Marjorie, The World of Orderic Vitalis (Oxford: Clarendon Press, 1984).

Follows a short biography of Orderic (1075-c. 1142) with surveys of the monastic and secular worlds, then concludes with an assessment of Orderic as historian in early twelfth-century society.

487. Constable, Giles, "Renewal and Reform in Religious Life: Concepts and Realities," in R. Benson and G. Constable, eds., Renaissance and Renewal in the Twelfth Century (Cambridge, MA: Harvard University Press, 1982), 37-67.

Sees in the twelfth century a movement "from what may be called a backward- to a forward-looking ideology of reform." Concentrates on the tendency of twelfth-century religious reformers to look more to future needs than to the past for ideal models and concludes that comparable optimism concerning institutional change for the better permeates the century's thinking.

488. Cowdrey, H.E., The Age of Abbot Desiderius: Montecassino, the Papacy, and the Normans in the Eleventh and Early Twelfth Centuries (Oxford: Clarendon Press, 1983).

Focuses on one religious house and one abbot who later became pope (Victor III, 1086-87), but the author's assessments of Montecassino and Desiderius have a broader application than this house and abbot alone. Accompanying bibliography is lengthy but narrow.

489. Cricco, Patricia, "Monasticism and its Role as a Liminal Community in Medieval Society." Ph.D. dissertation: West Virginia University, 1981.
Uses the anthropological model of ritual liminality. Concludes eleventh- and twelfth-century monasticism successively used withdrawal from society and mendicant "witness" to develop a spirituality better suited for the new social conditions of the central Middle Ages.

490. De Pinto, Basil, "The Twelfth-Century Benedictines and Cistercian Monasticism," Cistercian Studies, 4(1969), 177-88.
Discusses the nature and major issues of the Benedictine-Cistercian controversy, and the conflict between Peter the Venerable (1092-1156) and Bernard of Clairvaux (1090-1153).

491. Greenway, Diana et al., eds., Tradition and Change: Essays in Honour of Marjorie Chibnall Presented by Her Friends on the Occasion of Her Seventieth Birthday (Cambridge, England: Cambridge University Press, 1985).
Fourteen articles in two sections. "Ecclesiastical Themes" includes C. Holdsworth, "Orderic, Traditional Monk and the New Monasticism"; G. Constable, "Baume and Cluny in the Twelfth Century"; and R. Foreville, "Canterbury et la canonisation des saints au XIIe siècle." "Secular Themes" includes M. Cheney, "A Decree of King Henry II on Defect of Justice" and D. Clementi, "Constitutional Development Through Pressure of Circumstance."

492. Hill, Bennett D., English Cistercian Monasteries and Their Patrons in the Twelfth Century (Urbana: University of Illinois Press, 1968).
Chapters on the beginnings of Cistercianism in England, Cistercian patrons, the congregation of Savigny, and the Cistercians in the latter decades of the Gregorian Reform. Of special interest are considerations of who in successive generations contributed to and enlisted in the English Cistercian movement.

493. Leclercq, Jean, "The Monastic Crisis of the 11th and 12th Centuries," in N. Hunt, ed., Cluniac Monasticism in the Central Middle Ages (London: Macmillan, 1971), 217-37.
   Perceives an essentially spiritual crisis in monasticism in the late eleventh and early twelfth centuries. The crisis was precipitated by the overconfidence and overextension of the Benedictines, plus an ascetic movement that produced several formidable institutional rivals. The result served to purify and to strengthen monastic traditions by the end of the twelfth century.

494. ------, "Consciousness of Identification in 12th Century Monasticism," Cistercian Studies, 14(1979), 219-31.
   Challenges to monasticism as the premier mode of religious life and increased diversity within monasticism itself caused within twelfth-century monastic circles a collective reassessment of the monastic identity. Theology and literary, psychological, and sociological anayses are used in this appraisal of the process.

495. ------, Monks and Love in Twelfth-Century France: Psycho-Historical Essays (Oxford: Oxford University Press, 1979).
   A collection of essays that applies the framework for psychohistorical research set down by Leclercq in "Modern Psychology and the Interpretation of Medieval Texts," Speculum, 48(1973), 476-90; and "Modern Psychology and the Understanding of Medieval People," Cistercian Studies, 11(1976), 269-89. Topics here include "Modern Psychology and the Medieval Psyche," "New Recruitment--New Psychology," "Aggressiveness or Repression in St. Bernard and in His Monks," and "Champagne as a Garden of Love." See related item 460 in section 4.1

496. Leyser, Henrietta, Hermits and the New Monasticism: A Study of Religious Communities in Western Europe, 1000-1150 (London: Macmillan, 1984).
   Traces the development, methods of organization, and observances of the "new" hermits (itinerant holy men, as compared to traditional solitary hermits), placing them in the context of twelfth-century religious foment and the

proliferation of new monastic orders. Substantial bibliography.

497. Lynch, Joseph H., "Monastic Recruitment in the Eleventh and Twelfth Centuries: Some Social and Economic Considerations," American Benedictine Review, 26(1975), 425-47.
Studies the "repetitive social event" of entry into religious life in the twelfth century, discussing the elements of personal qualifications, offerings by entrants, negotiations, economic advantages, and litigation in this consideration of a symbiotic relationship between religious houses and the lay nobility.

498. Southern, Richard W., St. Anselm and His Biographer: A Study of Monastic Life and Thought, 1059-c. 1130 (Cambridge, England: Cambridge University Press, 1963).
Views Anselm's life and thought in their own right but also uses Anselm and his biographer as a vehicle for larger considerations of contemporary thought and society. A principal consideration in the latter regard is the place of monasticism in the early twelfth century.

499. Van Engen, John, "The 'Crisis' of Cenobitism Reconsidered: Benedictine Monasticism in the Years 1050-1150," Speculum, 61(1986), 269-304.
Counters the long-standing view that monasticism experienced a crisis in the eleventh and twelfth centuries as evidenced by the proliferation of new orders in apparent response to a Benedictine decline. Extensive review of the state of Benedictinism concludes it experienced no internal "crisis," did not suffer from institutional or spiritual "decadence," and indeed participated in contemporary reform movements.

4.2 Additional Works

500. Benton, John F., "The Personality of Guibert of Nogent," Psychoanalytic Review, 57(1971), 562-86.
501. Bouton, Jean de la Croix, Bibliographie bernardine, 1891-1957 (Paris: P. Lethielleux, 1958).

502. Bredero, Adriaan H., Cluny et Citeaux au douzième siècle: l'histoire d'une controverse monastique (Amsterdam: APA-Holland University Press, 1985).
503. ------, "The Conflicting Interpretations of the Relevance of Bernard of Clairvaux to the History of His Own Time," Citeaux, 31(1980), 53-81.
504. Brown, R. Allen, "England in Europe: The Norman Impact," History Today, 36:2(February 1986), 8-16.
505. Constable, Giles, Medieval Monasticism: A Select Bibliography (Toronto: University of Toronto Press, 1976).
506. ------, "Liberty and Free Choice in Monastic Thought and Life, Specially in the Eleventh and Twelfth Century," in G. Makdisi et al., eds., La notion de liberté au Moyen Age, Islam, Byzance, Occident (Paris: Belles lettres, 1985), 99-118.
507. Coupe, Michael D., "The Personality of Guibert de Nogent Reconsidered," Journal of Medieval History, 9(1983), 317-29.
508. D'Haenens, Albert, "Quotidienneté et contexte: pour un modèle d'interprétation de la réalité monastique médiévale (XIe-XIIe siècles)," Istituzioni monastiche e istituzione canonicali in occidente (1123-1215) (Milan: Vita e pensiero, 1980), 567-600.
509. Dronke, Peter, Abelard and Heloise in Medieval Testamonies (Glasgow: University of Glasgow Press, 1976).
510. Dubois, Jacques, Histoire monastique en France au XIIe siècle: le institutions monastiques et leur évolution (London: Variorum Reprints, 1982).
511. Duby, Georges, "Les chanoines réguliers et la vie économique des XIe et XIIe siècles," Hommes et structures du Moyen Age (Paris: Mouton, 1973), 203-12.
512. Elm, Kaspar, ed., Norbert von Xanten: Adliger, Ordenstifter, Kirchenfürst (Cologne: Wienand, 1984).
513. Evans, Gillian R., The Mind of St. Bernard of Clarivaux (Oxford: Oxford University Press, 1983).
514. Foreville, Raymonde, "Tradition et renouvellement du monachisme dans l'espace Plantagenet au XIIe s.," Cahiers de civilisation médiévale, 29(1986), 61-73.
515. Hallier, A., Un éducateur monastique: Aelred de Rievaulx (Paris: J. Gabalda, 1959). Translated by C. Heaney as The

Monastic Theology of Ailred of Rievaulx (Shannon, England: Irish University Press, 1969).

516. Kantor, Jonathan, "A Psychohistorical Source: The Memoirs of Abbot Guibert of Nogent," Journal of Medieval History, 2(1976), 281-303.

517. Knowles, David, The Monastic Order in England, 943-1216, 2d ed. (Cambridge, England: Cambridge University Press, 1966).

518. ------, "St. Bernard of Clairvaux, 1090-1153," The Historian and Character and Other Essays (Cambridge, England: Cambridge University Press, 1963), 31-49.

519. ------, "Cistercians and Cluniacs: The Controversy Between St. Bernard and Peter the Venerable," The Historian and Character and Other Essays (Cambridge, England: Cambridge University Press, 1963), 50-75.

520. Lackner, Bede K., The Eleventh-Century Background of Citeaux (Washington, DC: Cistercian Publications, 1972).

521. Lawrence, Hugh, "England in Europe, 1066-1453: The Monastic Revival," History Today, 36:3(March 1986), 27-33.

522. Leclercq, Jean, L'amour des lettres et le désir de Dieu (Paris: Cerf, 1957). Translated by C. Misrahi as The Love of Learning and the Desire for God, 3d ed. (New York: Fordham University Press, 1982).

523. ------, "Literature and Psychology in Bernard of Clairvaux," Downside Review, 93(1975), 1-20.

524. ------, Le mariage vu par les moines au XIIe siècle (Paris: Cerf, 1983).

525. Lekai, Louis J., The Cistercians: Ideals and Reality (Kent, OH: Kent State University Press, 1977).

526. ------, "Motive and Ideals of the Eleventh-Century Monastic Renewal," Cistercian Studies, 4(1969), 3-20.

527. Longère, Jean, La prédication médiévale (Paris: Etudes augustiniennes, 1983).

528. McGuire, Brian P., "The Cistercians and the Transformation of Monastic Friendship," Analecta cisterciensia, 37(1983 for 1981), 3-65.

529. Milis, Ludo, "Ermites et chanois réguliers au XIIe siècle," Cahiers de civilisation médiévale, 22(1979), 39-80.

530. Moolenbroek, J.J. van, <u>Vitalis van Savigny (d. 1122): bronnen en vroege cultus</u> (Amsterdam: Academische Pers, 1982).
531. Pennington, M. Basil, <u>The Last of the Fathers: The Cistercian Fathers of the Twelfth Century: A Collection of Essays</u>, Studies in Monasticism, 1 (Still River, MA: St. Bede's Publications, 1983).
532. Racinet, Philippe, "Implantation et expansion clunisiennes au nord-est de Paris (XIe-XIIe siècles)," <u>Moyen Age</u>, 39(1984), 5-37.
533. Renna, Thomas J., "Early Cistercian Attitudes Towards War in Historical Perspective," <u>Citeaux</u>, 31(1980), 119-29.
534. ------, "Abelard vs. Bernard: An Event in Monastic History," <u>Citeaux</u>, 27(1976), 189-202.
535. Riché, Pierre, "L'enfant dans la société monastique au XIIe siècle," in <u>Pierre Abélard, Pierre le Vénérable: les courants philosophiques, littéraires et artistiques en occident au milieu du XIIe siècle</u> (Paris: Centre national de la recherche scientifique, 1975), 689-701.
536. Rosenwein, Barbara H., "Feudal Warfare and Monastic Peace: Cluniac Liturgy as Ritual Aggression," <u>Viator</u>, 2(1971), 129-57.
537. Schneider, Ambrosius, <u>Die Cistercienser: Geschichte, Geist, Kunst</u> (Cologne: Wienand, 1974).
538. Squire, Aelred, <u>Aelred of Rievaulx: A Study</u> (London: Society for the Preservation of Christian Knowledge, 1969).

4.2 Related Items

<u>Section 2.1.2</u>: 129; <u>section 2.3</u>: 196; <u>section 4.1</u>: 456, 459-461, 470, 475, 461; <u>section 4.2</u>: 508; <u>section 4.3.2</u>: 579, 605; <u>section 4.3.5</u>: 649; <u>section 4.4.2</u>: 672; <u>section 4.5</u>: 788.

4.3 Learning and Intellectual Life

4.3.1 General

539. Baldwin, John W., <u>Masters, Princes, and Merchants: The Social Views of Peter the Chanter and His Circle</u>, 2 vols. (Princeton: Princeton University Press, 1970).
   Examines the intellectual relationships among Peter the Chanter (d. 1189), Stephen Langton (c. 1150-1228), Gerald of Wales (1147-1223), and others at the University of Paris. Describes the schools and academic life at Paris, then assesses the influence of their studies on society. Volume two contains appendices and 233 pages of notes to volume one.

540. Bautier, Robert H., ed., <u>La France de Philippe Auguste: le temps de mutation: actes du Colloque international, Paris, 1980</u> (Paris: Centre national de la recherche scientifique, 1982).
   Fifty papers presented to a 1980 conference includes the section "Les mutations intellectuelles: l'enseignement et la pensée" with papers by J. Verger ("Des écoles à l'université: la mutation institutionelle"), J. Chatillon ("Le mouvement théologique dans la France de Philippe Auguste"), and R. Manselli ("Spiritualité et hétérodoxie en France au temps de Philippe Auguste").

541. Beddie, James S., "Libraries in the Twelfth Century: Their Catalogues and Contents," in C.H. Taylor, ed., <u>Anniversary Essays in Medieval History by Students of Charles Homer Haskins</u> (Boston: Houghton Mifflin,, 1929), 1-23.
   Discusses the use of library catalogs as sources for intellectual history, the growth of libraries in the twelfth century, and library catalogs as gauges of twelfth-century culture.

542. Bryer, Anthony, "Cultural Relations Between East and West in the Twelfth Century," in D. Baker, ed., <u>Relations Between East and West in the Middle Ages</u> (Edinburgh: Edinburgh University Press, 1973), 77-94.
   Cultural exchange between Byzantium and the Latin West was quite limited. Byzantine intellectuals grew increasingly

anti-Latin during the twelfth century, and Greeks and Latins were fundamentally uninterested in one another. See related items 249 and 256 in section 3.1.

543. D'Alverny, Marie T., "Translations and Translators," in R. Benson and G. Constable, eds., Renaissance and Renewal in the Twelfth Century (Cambridge, MA: Harvard University Press, 1982), 421-62.
Surveys and discusses the contributions of these intermediaries in the renewal of learning in the twelfth century under the rubrics of "The Forerunners," "The Twelfth Century," "Translations from Arabic," "Translations in Spain," and "Diffusion of the Translations."

544. Grabois, Aryeh, "The Hebraica veritas and Jewish-Christian Intellectual Relations in the Twelfth Century," Speculum, 50(1975), 613-34.
Growing urban centers of the twelfth century provided opportunities for substantial and lively intellectual exchanges between Jews and Christians. Beginning at scholarly centers like St. Victor, these exchanges focused initially on biblical studies but extended to other subjects and frequently transcended scholarly pursuits to include social interaction.

545. Guth, Klaus, Johannes von Salisbury (1115/20-1180): Studien zur Kirchen-, Kultur- und Sozialgeschichte Westeuropas im 12. Jahrhunderts (St. Ottilien: Eos, 1978).
An overview of the twelfth-century environment for the study of philosophy. Guth does here for John of Salisbury (c. 1115-1180) what R.W. Southern does for Anselm in item 498.

546. McKeon, Richard, "The Organization of Sciences and the Relations of Cultures in the Twelfth and Thirteenth Centuries," in J. Murdoch and E. Sylla, eds., The Cultural Context of Medieval Learning: Proceedings of the First International Colloquium on Philosophy, Science, and Theology in the Middle Ages, 1973 (Boston: D. Reidel, 1975), 151-84.
Views the confluence of four cultures (classical Greek, classical Roman, medieval Arabic, and Latin Christian) in

the formation of the medieval Western encyclopedic tradition. This tradition to a great extent established the lines of demarcation among academic disciplines and the internal structures of those disciplines as they developed in the twelfth and thirteenth centuries.

547. McLaughlin, Mary M., "Abelard as Autobiographer: The Motives and Meaning of His Story of Calamities," Speculum, 42(1967), 463-88.

By no means a complete biography, rather an examination of Abelard's (1079-1142) autobiography--and by extension his life, particularly the psychological conditions under which the autobiography was written.

548. Pierre Abélard, Pierre le Vénérable: les courants philosophiques, littéraires et artistiques en occident au milieu du XIIe siècle. Colloques internationaux du Centre National de la Recherche Scientifique, 1972 (Paris: Centre national de la recherche scientifique, 1975).

Papers vary considerably in length and substance, and many go well beyond the limits of these two Peters. Several contributions are useful principally for bibliographic purposes.

549. Rouse, Richard H. and M. Rouse, "Statim invenire: Schools, Preachers, and New Attitudes to the Page," in R. Benson and G. Constable, eds., Renaissance and Renewal in the Twelfth Century (Cambridge, MA: Harvard University Press, 1982), 201-25.

The late twelfth century experienced a transformation in the tools of scholarship. The transition from memory to the page, and the dramatic expansion in the corpus of scholarly literature, led to the development of various finding devices and other scholarly apparatus that contributed to the formalization of pedagogical methods. See related items 30 in section 1.1, and 658 and 663 in section 4.4.1.

550. Sikes, Jeffrey G., Peter Abailard (Cambridge, England: Cambridge University Press, 1932).

Sorely out of date but the most scholarly biography of one of the more controversial figures of the twelfth century.

551. Smalley, Beryl, The Becket Conflict and the Schools: A Study of Intellectuals in Politics (Oxford: B. Blackwell, 1973).
Provides an intellectual, and to a lesser extent a social and political, background to the Becket conflict. Chapters on various participants weigh the motivational and intellectual aspects of their participation in the debate. See related items 213, 222, 230, and 263 in section 3.1.

552. ------, "The Gospels in the Paris Schools in the Late 12th and Early 13th Centuries: Peter the Chanter, Hugh of St. Cher, Alexander of Hales, John of La Rochelle," Franciscan Studies, 39(1979), 230-54; 40(1980), 298-369.
Compares the gospel teaching of a secular master and three mendicants, all of whom were active in the Parisian schools when the concept of the vita apostolica became a critical concern among academics.

553. Verger, Jacques and Jean Jolivet, Bernard/Abélard: ou, le cloître et l'école (Paris: Fayard-Mame, 1982).
Focuses on Bernard of Clairvaux (1090-1153) but treats Abelard (1079-1142) fairly. Chief value lies in the concluding summary of the historical importance of these major figures.

554. Wilks, Michael, ed., The World of John of Salisbury (Oxford: B. Blackwell, 1984).
A collection of 25 essays that study John of Salisbury (c. 1115-1180) in his own right and as a vehicle for the discussion of larger questions. Articles include C. Brooke, "John of Salisbury and His World"; D. Luscombe, "John of Salisbury in Recent Scholarship"; P. Riché, "Jean de Salisbury et le monde scolaire du XIIè siècle"; and D. Luscombe, "John of Salisbury: A Bibliography, 1953-82."

4.3.1 Additional Works

555. Baldwin, John W., The Scholastic Culture of the Middle Ages, 1000-1300 (Lexington, MA: D.C. Heath, 1971).
556. Bartlett, Robert J., Gerald of Wales, 1146-1223 (Oxford: Clarendon Press, 1982).

557. Clanchy, M.T., "Moderni in Education and Government in England," Speculum, 50(1975), 671-88.
558. Eberhard, Winfried, "Ansätze zur Bewältigung ideologischer Pluralität im 12. Jahrhundert: Pierre Abelard und Anselm von Havelberg," Historisches Jahrbuch, 105(1985), 353-87.
559. Flint, Valerie I., "The Place and Purpose of the Works of Honorius Augustodunensis," Revue bénédictine, 87(1977), 97-127.
560. Grane, Leif, Peter Abelard: Philosophy and Christianity in the Middle Ages (London: Allen & Unwin, 1970).
561. Häring, Nikolaus M., "Auctoritas in der sozialen und intellektuellen Struktur des zwölften Jahrhunderts," in A. Zimmerman, ed., Soziale Ordnungen im Selbstverständnis des Mittelalters (Berlin: W. de Gruyter, 1980), 517-33.
562. Jackson, Sidney L., "The Twelfth Century in the West, its Libraries, and Hugh of St. Victor's Classification of Knowledge," Journal of Library History, 2(1967), 185-200.
563. Luscombe, David E., Peter Abelard (London: Historical Association, 1979).
564. McLachlan, Elizabeth P., The Scriptorium of Bury St. Edmunds in the Twelfth Century (New York: Garland, 1986). [Reprint of a 1965 dissertation.]
565. Moore, R.I., "Guibert of Nogent and His World," in H. Mayr-Harting and R.I. Moore, eds., Studies in Medieval History Presented to R.H.C. Davis (London: Hambledon Press, 1985), 107-17.
566. Orme, Nicholas, From Childhood to Chivalry: The Education of English Kings and Aristocracy, 1066-1530 (London: Methuen, 1984).
567. Richter, Michael, Giraldus Cambrensis: The Growth of the Welsh Nation, rev. ed. (Aberystwyth: National Library of Wales, 1976).
568. ------, "Gerald of Wales: A Reassessment on the 750th Anniversary of His Death," Traditio, 29(1973), 379-90.
569. Roberts, Brynley F., Gerald of Wales (Cardiff: University of Wales Press, 1982).
570. Robertson, Jr., Durant W., Abelard and Heloise (New York: Dial Press, 1972).
571. Sommerfeldt, John R., "Bernard of Clairvaux and Scholasticism," Papers of the Michigan Academy of Science, Arts, and Letters, 48(1963), 265-77.

572. Steinen, Wolfram von den, "Natur und Geist im zwölften Jahrhundert," Die Welt als Geschichte, 14(1954), 71-90.
573. Stollberg, Gunnar, Die soziale Stellung der intellektuellen Obersicht im England des 12. Jahrhunderts (Lübeck: Matthiesen, 1973).
574. Thomson, Rodney M., "The Library of Bury St. Edmunds Abbey in the Eleventh and Twelfth Centuries," Speculum, 47(1972), 617-45.
575. Williams, E.A., "A Bibliography of Giraldus Cambrensis," National Library of Wales Journal, 12(1961-62), 97-140.

4.3.1 Related Entries

Section 1.1: 1, 7, 11, 13, 17, 20, 28, 31, 37; section 2.1.2: 134; section 3.1: 270; section 3.3: 381, 382, 386; section 3.4: 421; section 4.1: 460; section 4.2: 486; section 4.3.2: 588, 589, 597, 602; section 4.3.3: 609, 613, 614; section 4.3.4: 622-625, 628, 632, 634; section 4.3.5: 641, 642, 644, 650, 652, 653; section 4.4.2: 676, 692, 707, 717.

4.3.2 Theology and Philosophy

576. Chenu, Marie D., La théolgoie au douzième siècle (Paris: J. Vrin, 1957). Selections translated by J. Taylor and L. Little as Nature, Man, and Society in the Twelfth Century: Essays on New Theological Perspectives in the Latin West (Chicago: University of Chicago Press, 1968).

This is the essential Chenu, a study that has been hailed as the most important work on medieval intellectual history since World War II. This translation retains Chenu's vision of a dynamic theology in its social and cultural context.

577. Cloes, Henry, "La systématisation théologique pendant la première moitié du XIIe siècle," Ephemerides theologicae louvanienses, 34(1958), 277-329.

Studies the major theological works from the School of Laon through Peter Lombard's Book of Sentences (1150), paying special attention to authors' regard for the notion of synthesis and reconciliation, and the means they employed in attempting to achieve it. Includes extensive primary and secondary references.

578. Davy, Marie M., Initiation médiévale: la philosophie au douzième siècle (Paris: A. Michel, 1980).

A broad yet insightful survey of twelfth-century philosophy in four sections: background that includes a discussion of twelfth-century originality, the sources of twelfth-century philosophy, intellectual and institutional structure of philosophy, and overviews of the prophetic, ascetic, and monastic philosophies of the period.

579. Déchanet, Jean M., Guillaume de Saint-Thierry: l'homme et son oeuvre (Paris: A. et J. Picard, 1972). Translated by R. Strachan as William of St. Thierry: The Man and His Work (Spencer, MA: Cistercian Publications, 1972).

Concluding chapters on twelfth-century monasticism and theology place William (c. 1085-1148), one of the century's more under-rated intellectuals, in a larger context. The bibliography has been updated with the translation but remains sparse.

580. Evans, Gillian R., Old Arts and New Theology: The Beginnings of Theology as an Academic Discipline (Oxford: Clarendon Press, 1980).

Analyzes the emergence of theology as an academic discipline in the urban schools, supplanting the monasteries as centers of theological study. Also important is the establishment of theology as a "science."

581. ------, "The Borrowed Meaning: Grammar, Logic, and the Problem of Theological Language in Twelfth-Century Schools," Downside Review, 96(1978), 165-75.

The degree of interest scholars hold for the theory of language can be an indication of the degree of subtlety in their philosophical and theological investigations. This study considers the increased interest in grammar and logic in the twelfth century, assesses its implications for theological studies, and notes the contributions of several grammarians, logicians, and theologians.

582. Foreville, Raymonde, ed., <u>Le mutations socio-culturelles au tournant des XIe-XIIe siècles; études anselmiennes (IVe session: colloque, Abbaye Notre Dame du Bec, 1982</u> (Paris: Centre national de la recherche scientifique, 1984).
Forty-seven papers plus discussions. Contributions include J. Brundage, "Anselm, Ivo of Chartres and the Ideology of the the First Crusade"; J. Chatillon, "Saint Anselme et l'écriture"; and R. Campbell, "The Systematic Character of Anselm's Thought."

583. Gersh, Stephen, "Platonism--Neoplatonism--Aristotelianism: A Twelfth-Century Metaphysical System and its Sources," in R. Benson and G. Constable, eds., <u>Renaissance and Renewal in the Twelfth Century</u> (Cambridge, MA: Harvard University Press, 1982), 512-34.
An important twelfth-century commentary on Boethius's <u>De trinitate</u> is analyzed for its Platonic, Neoplatonic, and Aristotelian content. Concludes that the twelfth century inherited and transmitted a substantial body of Platonic thought beyond the limited number of works attributed to Plato and available at that time.

584. Ghellinck, Joseph de, <u>Le mouvement théologique du XIIe siècle</u>, 2d ed. (Brussells: Culture et civilisation, 1969).
Peter Lombard (1100-1160) is the major figure in this classic survey of twelfth-century theology. Two of five chapters and a majority of the lengthy book's pages are devoted to him. Other chapters discuss the periods just prior to and following Peter Lombard, and general aspects of theology and canon law in the period.

585. Gross, Charlotte, "Twelfth-Century Concepts of Time: Three Reinterpretations of Augustine's Doctrine of Creation <u>simul</u>," <u>Journal of the History of Philosophy</u>, 23(1985), 325-38.
Uses Augustinian notion of <u>simul</u> to gauge twelfth-century concepts of time. Argues Chartrians developed greater sensitivity to time, sequence, and process; Victorines

viewed time as related to spiritual progress; and together they represent a new awareness of time.

586. Hödl, L, "Die dialektische Theologie des 12. Jahrhunderts," in <u>Arts libéraux et philosophie du Moyen Age: actes du quatrième Congrès international de philosophie médiévale, 1967</u> (Paris: J. Vrin, 1969).

Draws on the work of Peter Abelard (1079-1142), Gilbert of Poitiers (1076-1154), and Odo of Soissons (twelfth century) for illustrations of the dialectical method that became popular in twelfth-century theology.

587. Leclercq, Jean, "The Renewal of Theology," in R. Benson and G. Constable, eds., <u>Renaissance and Renewal in the Twelfth Century</u> (Cambridge, MA: Harvard University Press, 1982), 68-87.

Portrays the theological renewal of the twelfth century, from around 1075 to about 1224, as more of an intensification and diversification than a renewal <u>per se</u>. In this period separate theologies developed in the monasteries and the schools, each with different audiences, theological concerns, intellectual methods, and modes of expression.

588. Le Goff, Jacques, <u>La naissance du purgatoire</u> (Paris: Gallimard, 1981). Translated by A. Goldhammer as <u>The Birth of Purgatory</u> (Chicago: University of Chicago Press, 1984).

Investigates the twelfth-century origin of the concept of purgatory from the perspectives of both theology and folklore. As is usual with this author, the study is interdisciplinary, far-reaching, and employs a wide variety of sources.

589. Luscombe, David E., <u>The School of Peter Abelard: The Influence of Abelard's Thought in the Early Scholastic Period</u> (London: Cambridge University Press, 1969).

Two condemnations prevented Abelard (1079-1142) from founding a formal school of theology, but his influence on medieval theology remained substantial. Luscombe isolates Abelard's theological contributions, considers their reception and transmittal by his students, and compares these contributions with the schools of Laon and St. Victor.

590. Nielson, Lauge O., Theology and Philosophy in the Twelfth Century: A Study of Gilbert Porreta's Thinking and the Theological Expositions of the Doctrine of Incarnation during the Period 1130-1180 (Leiden: E.J. Brill, 1982).
A technical study of Gilbert of Poitiers's (1076-1154) doctrine of the incarnation. Provides an account of one intellectual's reconciliation of philosophy and theology, and a survey of contemporary theologian-philosophers that includes Hugh of St. Victor (1096-1141), Peter Abelard (1079-1142), and Peter Lombard (1100-1160). The bibliography is substantial but narrow.

4.3.2 Additional Works

591. Baldwin, John W., The Medieval Theories of the Just Price: Romanists, Canonists, and Theologians in the Twelfth and Thirteenth Centuries, Transactions of the American Philosophical Society, 49 (Philadelphia: American Philosophical Soceity, 1959).
592. Chenu, Marie D., "Un essai de méthode théologique au XIIe siècle," Revue sciences philosophiques et théologiques, 24(1935), 258-67.
593. Dales, Richard C., "Discussions of the Eternity of the World during the First Half of the Twelfth Century," Speculum, 57(1982), 495-508.
594. Delhaye, Philippe, Pierre Lombard: sa vie, ses oeuvres, sa morale (Paris: J. Vrin, 1961).
595. Dotto, Gianni, Il secolo XII: illuminismo logico e umanesimo del limite (Rome: Edizioni studium, 1978).
596. Ehlers, Joachim, "Arca significat ecclesiam: ein theologisches Weltmodell aus der ersten Hälfte des 12. Jahrhunderts," Frühmittelalterliche Studien, 6(1972), 171-87.
597. Elswijk, H.C. van, Gilbert Porreta: sa vie, son oeuvre, sa pensée (Leuven: Spicilegium sacrum louvaniense, 1966).
598. Evans, Gillian R., Alan of Lille: The Frontiers of Theology in the Later Twelfth Century (Cambridge, England: Cambridge University Press, 1983).
599. Gilson, Etienne H., La théologie mystique de Saint Bernard (Paris: J. Vrin, 1934). Translated by A. Downes as The

Mystical Theology of Saint Bernard (New York: Sheed & Ward, 1940).
600. Gracia, J. Introduction to the Problem of Individuation in the Early Middle Ages (Washington, DC: Catholic University of America Press, 1984).
601. Häring, Nikolaus M., Life and Works of Clarembald of Arras, a Twelfth-Century Master of the School of Chartres (Toronto: Pontifical Institute of Mediaeval Studies, 1965).
602. Javelet, Robert, Image et ressemblance au douzième siècle, de Saint Anselme à Alain de Lille, 2 vols. (Paris: Letouzey et Ane, 1967).
603. Lottin, D.O., Psychologie et morale aux XIIe et XIIIe siècles, 6 vols. (Louvain: Abbaye du Mont Cesar, 1942-1960).
604. MacKinnon, Hugh, "Theological Thought at the End of the Twelfth Century," Historical Reflections, 6(1979), 335-41.
605. Penco, Gregorio, "La teologia monastica: bilancio di un dibattito," Benedictina, 26(1979), 189-98.
606. Southern, Richard W., "St. Anselm," Medieval Humanism and Other Studies (Oxford: B. Blackwell, 1970), 9-18.
607. Wade, Francis, "Abelard and Individuality," in P. Wilpert, ed., Die Metaphysik im Mittelalter: ihr Ursprung und ihr Bedeutung (Berlin: W. de Gruyter, 1963), 165-71.
608. Widmer, Berthe, "Thierry von Chartres: ein Gelehrtenschicksal des 12. Jahrhunderts," Historische Zeitschrift, 200(1965), 552-71.

4.3.2 Related Entries

Section 1.1: 33; section 4.2: 498, 515; section 4.3.1: 543, 545, 548, 554; section 4.3.4: 629; section 4.3.5: 650, 653, 691; section 4.4.2: 708.

4.3.3 Biblical Studies and Exegesis

609. Bloomfield, Morton W., "Recent Scholarship on Joachim of Fiore and His Influence," in A. Williams, ed., Prophecy and Millenarianism: Essays in Honor of Marjorie Reeves (London: Longman, 1980), 21-52.
> Surveys work done (and considers work yet to be done) in several areas of Joachimite studies. Areas of discussion include Joachim's (c. 1132-1202) exegetical method, sources for his ideas, and his influence on others. Also see Bloomfield's "Joachim of Flora: A Critical Survey of his Canon, Teaching, Sources, Biography, and Influence," Traditio, 13(1957), 249-311.

610. Chatillon, Jean, "Les écoles du XIIe siècle," in P. Riché and G. Lobrichon, eds., Le Moyen Age et la Bible (Paris: Beauchesne, 1984), 163-97.
> A compact but detailed survey of biblical studies in twelfth-century schools. Suggests that commentary and exegesis underwent a transformation in this period as a part of a general spiritual renaissance beginning in the later eleventh century. Examples include several masters and the schools of Laon, Bec, and St. Victor.

611. Häring, Nikolaus M., "Commentary and Hermeneutics," in R. Benson and G. Constable, eds., Renaissance and Renewal in the Twelfth Century (Cambridge, MA: Harvard University Press, 1982), 173-200.
> Surveys titles of commentaries, the glosa ordinaria, the accessus ad auctores, important contributions of the abbey of St. Victor, and hermeneutics with special reference to twelfth-century developments. Bibliographical note included.

612. McGinn, Bernard J., The Calabrian Abbot: Joachim of Fiore in the History of Western Thought (New York: Macmillan, 1985).
> "Background to Joachim's Thought" (two chapters) details the influence of early Christian theologies of history and apocalyptic exegesis. "Main Themes of Joachim's Thought" (four chapters) explores such themes as Joachim as symbolist and his understanding of scripture. "In the Wake

of Joachim" (one chapter) is a comparative study of Joachim (c. 1132-1202), Thomas Aquinas (1224-74) and Bonaventure (c. 1217-74). Includes a critical bibliography.

613. Reeves, Marjorie, "The Originality and Influence of Joachim of Fiore," Traditio, 36(1980), 269-316.
Discusses the origins and later use of Joachim's (c. 1132-1202) major ideas and their relation to the work of contemporary thinkers.

614. Smalley, Beryl, The Study of the Bible in the Middle Ages, 3d ed. (Oxford: B. Blackwell, 1952).
The classic history of bible study in the central Middle Ages. Surveys the nature and techniques of biblical scholarship, as well as leading schools and scholars.

4.3.3 Additonal Works

615. Chenu, Marie D., "Nature ou histoire? Une controverse exégétique sur la creation au XIIe siècle," Archives d'histoire doctrinale et littéraire du Moyen Age, 28(1953), 25-30.
616. Flint, Valerie I., "Some Notes on the Early Twelfth Century Commentaries on the Psalms," Recherches de théologie ancienne et médiévale, 38(1971), 80-88.
617. Javelet, Robert, "Exégèse spirituelle aux XIe et XIIe siècles," in W. Kluxen et al., eds., Sprache und Erkenntnis im Mittelalter: Akten des VI. internationalen Kongresses für mittelalterliche Philosophie des Société internationale pour l'étude de la philosophie médiévale, 2 vols. (Berlin: W. de Gruyter, 1981), 2:873-80.
618. Leclercq, Jean, "Ecrits monastiques sur la Bible aux XIe-XIIIe siècles," Medieval Studies, 15(1953), 95-106.
619. Lerner, Robert, "Antichrists and Antichrist in Joachim of Fiore," Speculum, 60(1985), 553-70.
620. West, Delno C. and S. Zimdars-Swartz, Joachim of Fiore: A Study in Spiritual Perception and History (Bloomington, IN: Indiana University Press, 1983).

4.3.3 Related Entries

Section 4.3.1: 544, 552; section 4.3.4: 621.

4.3.4 Science and Natural Philosophy

621. Avi-Yonah, Reuven S., "The Aristotelean Revolution: A Study of the Transformation of Medieval Cosmology, 1150-1250." Ph.D. dissertation: Harvard University, 1986.

   Studies 40 commentaries on the creation composed at the University of Paris between 1150 and 1250. Concludes the university played a major role in advancing beyond Aristotle's cosmology, western intellectuals criticized Aristotle earlier than generally believed, and these developments are linked to the Scientific Revolution.

622. Beaujouan, Guy, "The Transformation of the Quadrivium," in R. Benson and G. Constable, eds., <u>Renaissance and Renewal in the Twelfth Century</u> (Cambridge, MA: Harvard University Press, 1982), 463-87.

   Assesses the profound impact of Arabic science on both the structure and the content of quadrivial studies. Copius notes refer to much primary material and a bibliographical note orients the reader to the leading secondary works on the history of the exact sciences in the twelfth century.

623. Dales, Richard C., "A Twelfth-Century Concept of the Natural Order," <u>Viator</u>, 9(1978), 179-92.

   Traces the development of a naturalistic attitude ("that nature is a self-sufficient, largely mechanical entity") from Adelard of Bath (c. 1070-after 1142) at the beginning of the twelfth century through Urso of Calabria and John Blunt at the beginning of the thirteenth.

624. D'Alverny, Marie T., "Le cosmos symbolique du XIIe siècle," <u>Archives d'histoire doctrinale et littéraire du Moyen Age</u>, 28(1953), 31-81.

Uses the works of Honorius Augustodunensis (c. 1080-1137), especially Clavis physicae, to illustrate the prevailing cosmological views of the twelfth century. Also discusses the derivation of Honorius's ideas, his debt to John Scotus Erigena (and by extenstion to the Greek fathers), and Honorius's relation to contemporaries.

625. Gregory, Tullio, "La nouvelle idée de nature et de savoir scientifique au XIIe siècle," in J. Murdoch and E. Sylla, eds., The Cultural Context of Medieval Learning: Proceedings of the First International Colloquium on Philosophy, Science, and Theology in the Middle Ages, Boston, 1973 (Boston: D. Reidel, 1975), 193-218.

Speaks generally of the appearance in the twelfth century of a new regard for nature that had a major impact on human thought and action. Of equal interest is an ensuing discussion of this and related questions by T. Gregory, R. McKeon, M. D'Alverny, B. Stock, and others.

626. Kealey, Edward J., Medieval Medicus: A Social History of Anglo-Norman Medicine (Baltimore: Johns Hopkins University Press, 1981).

Draws on academic, literary, and legal sources in this exposition of Anglo-Norman health care. Concentrates on the first half of the twelfth century, covering practitioners, institutions, and the practice of medicine itself. Extensive bibliography.

627. Stiefel, Tina, The Intellectual Revolution in Twelfth-Century Europe (London: Croom Helm, 1985).

Uses the work of three cosmologists--Adelard of Bath (c. 1070-after 1142), William of Conches (c. 1100-1154), and Thierry of Chartres (d. 1151)--to argue that "productive ideas concerning nature as a fit subject of objective inquiry were articulated in Western Europe before the appearance of the Aristotelian corpus in translation" (p. 2). Includes considerations of the influence of the new dialectic, the definition and study of science, analytical techniques, and regard for traditional knowledge. Also see her "Science, Reason, and Faith in the Twelfth Century: The

Cosmologists' Attack on Tradition," Journal of European Studies, 6(1976), 1-16.

628. Stiefel, Tina, "'Impious Men': Twelfth-Century Attempts to Apply Dialectic to the World of Nature," in P.O. Long, ed., Science and Technology in Medieval Society, Annals of the New York Academy of Sciences, 441 (New York: New York Academy of Sciences, 1985), 187-203.
>Assesses the implications of the emergence of a "rationalist, critical mode of thinking in the early twelfth century," focusing on "the actual reactions and repercussions that the movement awakened and the consequences for the men who initiated it." The initiators principally include William of Conches (c. 1100-1154), Thierry of Chartres (d. 1151), and Adelard of Bath (c. 1070-after 1142).

629. Stock, Brian, Myth and Science in the Twelfth Century: A Study of Bernard Silvester (Princeton: Princeton University Press, 1972).
>Centers on Bernard Silvester's mid-twelfth-century Cosmographia, an epic cosmogony in the tradition of Plato's Timaeus. Assesses the literary and mythological content of the work, rather than its scientific elements, and thereby provides general cultural and intellectual background for the study of twelfth-century science and natural philosophy.

630. White, Jr., Lynn, "Science and the Sense of Self: The Medieval Background of a Modern Confrontation," Daedalus, 107:2(Spring 1978), 47-59.
>Twelfth- and thirteenth-century transformations in spirituality (emergence of a humanized Christ in favor of a transcendant Creator God, a more intense personal piety, and the movement from a shame to a guilt culture), all evidencing the development of a self-awareness fundamental to the modern notion of science and a "scientific" regard for nature.

4.3.4 Additional Works

631. Crombie, A.C., Medieval and Early Modern Science, 2d ed. (Garden City, NY: Doubleday, 1959).

632. Evans, Gillian R., "The Influence of Quadrivium Studies in the 11th- and 12th-Century Schools," Journal of Medieval History, 1(1975), 151-64.

633. Haskins, Charles H., Studies in the History of Mediaeval Science (Cambridge, MA: Harvard University Press, 1924).

634. Lange, Hanne, Les données mathématiques des traités du XIIe siècle sur la symbolique des nombres (Copenhagen: Université de Copenhagen, 1979).

635. Stiefel, Tina, "The Heresy of Science: A Twelfth-Century Conceptual Revolution," Isis, 68(1977), 347-62.

636. ------, "Twelfth-Century Matter for Metaphor: The Material View of Plato's Timaeus," British Journal for the History of Science, 17(1984), 169-85.

637. Stock, Brian, "Rationality, Tradition, and the Scientific Outlook: Reflections on Max Weber and the Middle Ages," in P.O. Long, ed., Science and Technology in Medieval Society, Annals of the New York Academy of Sciences, 441 (New York: New York Academy of Sciences, 1985), 7-19.

638. Thuillier, P., "The Scientific Revolution in the Twelfth Century," Recherche, 13(1982), 1018-33.

4.3.4 Related Entries

Section 1.1: 33; section 2.1.2: 134.

4.3.5 The Universities and Schools

639. Baldwin, John W., "Masters at Paris from 1179 to 1215: A Social Perspective," in R. Benson and G. Constable, eds., Renaissance and Renewal in the Twelfth Century (Cambridge, MA: Harvard University Press, 1982), 138-72.

Studies the development of universities in their social context during the late twelfth and early thirteenth centuries. Discussions focus on "The Capetian Contribution," "Schools and Society," and "Personal Identity." Includes lists of masters, some quantitative data, and a bibliographical note.

640. Classen, Peter, Studium und Gesellschaft im Mittelalter, Schriften der Monumenta Germaniae Historica, 29 (Stuttgart: A. Hiersemann, 1983).

Comprised largely of papers on education and society in the twelfth century, particularly the social context of early French schools and prosopographical studies of legal scholars in Italian, Parisian, and English universities and their influence on legal institutions.

641. Delhaye, Philippe, "L'organisation scolaire au XIIe siècle," Traditio, 5(1947), 211-68.

Surveys the educational institutions of the twelfth century, focusing on their structure and on education as an institutional process. Reviews the nature and evolution of monastic schools, other church schools prior to the emergence of urban cathedral schools, cathedral schools, and the universities in the early years of development.

642. Ferruolo, Stephen C., The Origins of the University: The Schools of Paris and Their Critics, 1100-1215 (Stanford: Stanford University Press, 1985).

Analyzes the arguments of four groups of critics of the schools of Paris: monks (mostly Cistercian), humanists, satirists, and masters and other scholars in or near Paris. Concludes that these arguments contributed appreciably to the formation and regulation of the schools and ultimately the University of Paris.

643. Flint, Valerie I., "The 'School of Laon:' A Reconsideration," Recherches de théologie ancienne et médiévale, 43(1976), 9-110.

Reaffirms use of the phrase, "school at Laon," and challenges the notion of a school of Laon. To use the latter suggests exegetical and theological traditions that have not been substantiated and perpetuates misconceptions about the later history of the schools, including that at Laon.

644. Little, Lester K., "Intellectual Training and Attitudes Toward Reform, 1075-1150," in Pierre Abélard, Pierre le Vénérable: les courant philosophiques, littéraires et artistiques en occident au milieu du XII siècle. Colloques internationaux du Centre national de la recherche scientifique, 1972 (Paris: Centre national de la recherche scientifique, 1975), 235-49.

Compares the lives of 10 radical reformers with the lives of 10 moderate or conservative reformers. Concludes that "attendance at an urban school was the decisive factor in the creation of a radical religious reformer."

645. Southern, Richard W., "The Schools of Paris and the Schools of Chartres," in R. Benson and G. Constable, eds., Renaissance and Renewal in the Twelfth Century (Cambridge, MA: Harvard University Press, 1982), 113-37.

In an earlier work the author objected to what he regarded as an exaggeration of the importance of the "school" of Chartres in the development of scholastic culture. In this work he recounts portions of this debate, provides a bibliographic orientation to the principal arguments (including critiques of his position by N. Häring and P. Dronke), and continues the discussion with an analysis of the schools in Paris and Chartres in the context of the intellectual and social conditions of the time. See related item 691 in section 4.4.2.

4.3.5 Additional Works

646. Chatillon, Jean, "Abélard et les écoles," in Abélard en son temps: actes du Colloque international organisé à l'occasion casion du 9e centenaire de la naissance de Pierre Abélard (Paris: Belles lettres, 1981), 133-60.
647. Dronke, Peter, "New Approaches to the School of Chartres," Anuario de estudios medievales, 6(1969), 117-40.
648. Haskins, Charles H., The Rise of Universities (New York: H. Holt, 1923).
649. Hunt, Richard W., The Schools and the Cloister: The Life and Writings of Alexander Nequam (1157-1217) (Oxford: Clarendon Press, 1984).

650. Paré, Gérard M., A. Brunet, and P. Tremblay, La renaissance du XIIe siècle: les écoles et l'ensignement (Paris: J. Vrin, 1933).
651. Payen, Jean C., "L'utopie chez les Chartrains," Moyen Age, 90(1984), 383-400.
652. Rashdall, Hastings, The Universities of Europe in the Middle Ages, ed. by F. Powicke and A. Emden, 3 vols. (London: Oxford University Press, 1951).
653. Southern, Richard W., Platonism, Scholastic Method and the School of Chartres (Reading: University of Reading Press, 1979).
654. ------, "Humanism and the School of Chartres," Medieval Humanism and Other Studies (Oxford: B. Blackwell, 1970), 61-85.
655. ------, "Master Vacarius and the Beginning of an English Academic Tradition," in J. Alexander and M. Gibson, eds., Medieval Learning and Literature: Essays Presented to R.W. Hunt (Oxford: Clarendon Press, 1976), 257-86.
656. Wheeler, Penny McElroy, "The Twelfth-Century School of St. Victor." Ph.d. dissertation: University of Southern California, 1970.
657. Williams, John R., "The Cathedral School of Reims in the Time of Master Alberic, 1118-1136," Traditio, 20(1964), 93-114.

4.3.5 Related Entries

Section 1.1: 33, 40; section 2.1.2: 108; section 4.3.1: 551, 552, 566; section 4.3.2: 585, 590, 601, 608; section 4.3.3: 610, 614; section 4.3.4: 621; section 4.4.2: 676, 691, 692.

4.4 Language and Literature

4.4.1 General

658. Clanchy, M.T., From Memory to Written Record: England, 1066-1307 (Cambridge, MA: Harvard University Press, 1979).

The growth of literacy in England in the central Middle Ages was due to practical necessity created by the proliferation of written documents and records. Clanchy assesses the impact of literacy on various social groups and gauges both the immediate practical and the long-term cultural implications of these developments. See also items 30 in section 1.0 and 549 in section 4.3.1.

659. Dronke, Peter, "Profane Elements in Literature," in R. Benson and G. Constable, eds., Renaissance and Renewal in the Twelfth Century (Cambridge, MA: Harvard University Press, 1982), 569-92.

Both Latin and vernacular literature manifest toward the end of the twelfth century notable departures in their regard for the profane and the sacred. In both literatures authors tend to question things sacred and affirm things profane in ways and to extents distinctively different from preceding centuries. Includes a bibliographical note.

660. Richter, Michael, Sprache und Gesellschaft im Mittelalter: Untersuchungen zur mündlichen Kommunikation in England vor der Mitte des 11. bis zum Beginn des 14. Jahrhunderts (Stuttgart: A. Hiersemann, 1979).

Considers the linguistic aspects of oral communication, including a chapter on the twelfth century. At this time English was the principal language spoken by the lower classes as well as many others in higher levels of society; Latin was rarely other than a second or third language and French was a first language for the most part only for "foreigners."

661. Schirmer, Walter F. and U. Broich, Studien zum literarischen Patronat im England des 12. Jahrhundert (Cologne: Westdeutscher Verlag, 1962).

Consists of two separate studies: "Die kulturelle Rolle des englischen Hofes im 12. Jahrhundert" by Schirmer and "Heinrich II. als Patron der Literatur seiner Zeit" by Broich. The former assesses the cultural influence of the Anglo-Norman court and the latter focuses on a monarch who represents a turning point in the involvement of English rulers in the patronage of literary works. See related item 740 in section 4.4.3.

662. Stevens, Martin, "The Performing Self in Twelfth-Century Culture," Viator, 9(1978), 193-212.

The performing self, wherein the artist "is centrally concerned with the act of his own creation," fully develops in the twelfth century, especially in the autobiographical and prefatory writings and sculptoral self-portraits of the period.

663. Turner, Ralph V., "The miles literatus in Twelfth- and Thirteenth-Century England: How Rare a Phenomenon?" American Historical Review, 83(1978), 928-45.

Literate laypersons were not nearly such rare phenomena in the central Middle Ages as generally has been assumed. Laypersons could and did acquire educations at this time, and in significant numbers; the need for literacy, particularly for the transaction of legal and governmental business, increased the number of literates; and a sufficient number of literate knights were available to meet the growing demands of the royal government. See related items 30 in section 1.0 and 549 in section 4.3.1.

4.4.1 Additional Works

664. Ferrante, Joan M., Woman as Image in Medieval Literature from the Twelfth Century to Dante (New York: Columbia University Press, 1975).
665. Gurevich, Aaron J., "Oral and Written Culture of the Middle Ages: Two Peasant Visions of the Late Twelfth-Early Thirteenth Centuries," New Literary History, 16(1984), 51-66.
666. Kazhdan, Alexander, Studies on Byzantine Literature of the Eleventh and Twelfth Centuries (Cambridge, England: Cambridge University Press, 1984).
667. Lally, J.E., "Secular Patronage at the Court of King Henry II," Bulletin of the Institute of Historical Research, 49(1976), 159-84.
668. Loyn, H. R., "The Norman Conquest of the English Language," History Today, 30(1980), 35-39.

669. Payen, Jean C., "L'humanisme médiévale et la redécouverté de l'individu en Occident du XIIe siècle à la fin du XIIIe siècle," Les cahiers de Fontenay, 1(1975), 96-106.
670. Schlösser, Felix, Andreas Capellanus: seine Minnelehre und das christliche Weltbild des 12. Jahrhunderts, 2d ed. (Bonn: H. Bouvier, 1960).
671. Schmitt, Jean C., "Les traditions folkloriques dans la culture médiévale: quelques reflexions de méthode," Archives des Sciences Sociales des Religions, 52(1981), 5-20.

4.4.1 Related Entries

Section 1.1: 11, 30; section 4.1: 466; section 4.3.1: 543, 549; section 4.4.2: 688, 714; section 4.4.3: 736, 757; section 4.5: 774.

4.4.2 Latin

672. Bynum, Caroline Walker, "Jesus as Mother and Abbot as Mother: Some Themes in Twelfth-Century Cistercian Writing," Harvard Theological Review, 70(1977), 257-84.
   Use of maternal imagery in theological and ecclesiastical contexts increased in popularity in the twelfth century, especially among Cistercians, as monasticism and conceptions of monastic dependence and independence underwent fundamental changes. Reprinted in her Jesus as Mother: Studies in the Spirituality of the High Middle Ages (Berkeley: University of California Press, 1984).

673. Classen, Peter, "Res gestae, Universal History, Apocalypse: Visions of Past and Future," in R. Benson and G. Constable, eds., Renaissance and Renewal in the Twelfth Century (Cambridge, MA: Harvard University Press, 1982), 387-417.
   Surveys the works of Orderic Vitalis (1075-c. 1142), William of Malmesbury (c. 1090-c. 1142), and Italian urban analists as examples of res gestae; Siegebert of Gembloux (c. 1030-1112), Frutolf of Bamberg (d. 1103), and

Otto of Freising (c. 1112-1158) as representatives of universal history; and Rupert of Deutz (c. 1070-1129), Hugh of St. Victor (c. 1096-1141), Anselm of Havelberg (c. 1095-1158), Gerhoch of Reichersberg (1093-1169), and Joachim of Fiore (d. c. 1240). Includes a bibliographical note especially good for German works.

674. Dronke, Peter, Women Writers of the Middle Ages: A Critical Study of Texts from Perpetua (d. 203) to Marguerite Porete (d. 1310) (Cambridge, England: Cambridge University Press, 1984).
Surveys personal testimonies by women in Latin and Provencal verse, works that contain "the spontaneous movement of poetic answering, and the calculated movement of literary shaping."

675. ------, Poetic Individuality in the Middle Ages: New Departures in Poetry, 1100-1150 (Oxford: Clarendon Press, 1970).
Ruodlieb, Semiramis, Peter Abelard's Planctus, and Hildegard of Bingen's Ordo virtutum witness a twelfth-century fascination with linguistic and social individuality (not necessarily individuality in personality).

676. Ehlers, Joachim, Hugo von St. Viktor: Studien zum Geschichtsdenken und zur Geschichtsschreibung des 12. Jahrhunderts (Wiesbaden: F. Steiner, 1973).
Approaches the works of Hugh (1096-1141) and other Victorines from an Annales or Strukturgeschichte perspective, using the documents to analyze the broader intellectual context for history writing in the twelfth century. Includes a large bibliography.

677. Ferguson, Chris D., "Autobiography as Therapy: Guibert de Nogent, Peter Abelard, and the Making of Medieval Autobiography," Journal of Medieval and Renaissance Studies, 13(1983), 181-212.
Examines the autobiographies of Guibert of Nogent (1052-1130) and Peter Abelard (1079-1142) as forerunners of the modern genre. Argues these autobiographies are expressions of both individual crisis and catharsis, and increased sensitivity to self-awareness in twelfth-century culture and society.

678. Huling, Richard W., "English Historical Writing under the Early Angevin Kings, 1170-1210." Ph.D. dissertation: State University of New York, 1980.
> Assesses the intellectual environment of and relationships among three early Angevin chroniclers: Roger of Howden (d. 1201), Ralph de Diceto (d. 1206), and Gervase of Canterbury (d. c. 1200). Principally concerned with the impact of political and ecclesiastical centralization on the chroniclers and their place in the English chronicle tradition.

679. Lehmann, Paul J., "Die Vielgestalt das zwölften Jahrhunderts," Historische Zeitschrift, 178(1954), 225-50.
> Reviews the principal currents, both national and transnational, in the Latin literature of the twelfth century. Emphasizes new departures and the diversity of literary activity.

680. ------, "Autobiographies of the Middle Ages," Transactions of the Royal Historical Society, 5th ser., 3(1953), 41-52.
> Surveys the autobiographical works of St. Augustine (354-430), Otloh of St. Emmeram (c. 1010-c. 1070), Ratherius of Verona (c. 887-974), Suger of St. Denis (1081-1151), Guibert of Nogent (1052-1130), Peter Abelard (1079-1142), and Gerald of Wales (1147-1223).

681. Lejeune, Rita, "La femme dans les littératures francaise et occitane du XIe au XIIIe siècle," Cahiers de civilisation médiévale, 20(1977), 201-17.
> Provides general considerations of women authors, "feminine" literary genres, female patrons, and the image of woman in works by women.

682. Liebeschütz, Hans, "Das zwölfte Jahrhundert und die Antike," Archiv für Kulturgeschichte, 35(1953), 247-71.
> Classical ideas and cultural forms played important roles in the humanistic flowering of the late eleventh and early twelfth centuries. Prominent examples are the influence of Cicero on Ailred of Rievaulx (1109-1167), Platonism on the School of Chartres, and antique traditions of political philosophy on John of Salisbury (c. 1115-1180).

683. Martin, Janet, "Classicism and Style in Latin Literature," in R. Benson and G. Constable, eds., Renaissance and Renewal in the Twelfth Century (Cambridge, MA: Harvard University Press, 1982), 537-68.
   Analyzes twelfth-century literary theory, epistolary prose, historical prose, quantitative verse, and verse techniques, with reference to works by Peter the Venerable (1092-1156), William of Poitiers (c. 1020-1090), and others. Concludes that both grammatical and stylistic developments in the literature of this period are indicative of its literary renaissance. Bibliographical note included.

684. Moi, Toril, "Desire in Language: Andreas Capellanus and the Controversy of Courtly Love," in D. Aers, ed., Medieval Literature: Criticism, Ideology, and History (Brighton: Harvester Press, 1986).
   Reviews interpretations of Andreas's (12th century) De amore in section one ("Text and History: The Controversy of Courtly Love"), then offers a feminist critique of the work in section two ("Love, Jealousy, and Epistemology in the De amore").

685. Partner, Nancy F., Serious Entertainments: The Writing of History in Twelfth-Century England (Chicago: University of Chicago Press, 1977).
   Separate analyses of Henry of Huntingdon (c. 1084-1155), William of Newburgh (1136-c. 1198), and Richard of Devizes (fl. 1191) followed by general discussions of historical evidence, literary form, and Christian history. Sizable bibliography.

686. Ray, Roger D., "Medieval Historiography Through the Twelfth Century: Problems and Progress of Research," Viator, 5(1974), 33-59.
   Considers the element of genre and the influence of biblical and classical literature on twelfth-century history writing. Includes extensive bibliographical notes and concludes with comments on areas requiring additional research.

687. Schüppert, Helga, Kirchenkritik in der lateinischen Lyrik des 12. und 13. Jahrhunderts (Munich: W. Fink, 1972).
Considers author and audience, critical themes, and stylistic devices of this genre of Latin satire. Criticism centers on the venality of secular clergy but is expressed without rejecting the faith or the institution.

688. Steinen, Wolfram von den, "Humanismus um 1100," Archiv für Kulturgeschichte, 46(1964), 1-20.
The Latin poetry of Hildebert of Lavardin (1056-1133) serves as the model for a review of early twelfth-century literary humanism.

689. Thomson, Rodney M., "The Origins of Latin Satire in Twelfth Century Europe," Mittellateinisches Jahrbuch, 13(1978), 73-83.
A period of reform followed by one of consolidation, a larger audience of educated readers, the availability of ancient models, the appearance of a large student community, and a dramatic growth in the size and influence of bureaucracies contributed to the increased popularlity of Latin satire in this period.

690. Trout, John M., The Voyage of Prudence: The World View of Alan of Lille (Washington, DC: University Press of America, 1979).
The writings of Alan of Lille (1128-1203) provide an exceptional panorama of twelfth-century society. Explicates Anticlaudianus and other works to outline the social views and humanism of both their author and the author's contemporaries. Substantial bibliography included.

691. Wetherbee, Winthrop, Platonism and Poetry in the Twelfth Century: The Literary Influence of the School of Chartres (Princeton: Princeton University Press, 1972).
Studies three scholars--Bernard Silvester (mid-twelfth century), Alan of Lille (1128-1203), and Jean of Hanville (twelfth century)--for their poetic contributions to the twelfth century and the acquisition of their Platonism through the School of Chartres. See related item 645 in section 4.3.2.

4.4.2 Additonal Works

692. Baron, Roger, Science et sagesse chez Hugues de Saint-Victor (Paris: Lethielleux, 1957).
693. Bertini, Ferruccio, ed., Commedie latine del XII e XIII secolo, 4 vols. (Genoa: Université di Genova, 1983).
694. Bliese, John, "The Study of Rhetoric in the Twelfth Century," Quarterly Journal of Speech, 63(1977), 364-83.
695. Brett, Martin, "John of Worcester and His Contemporaries," in R. Davis et al., eds., The Writing of History in the Middle Ages: Essays Presented to Richard William Southern (Oxford: Clarendon Press, 1981), 101-26.
696. Brooke, Christopher N., "Geoffrey of Monmouth as a Historian," in C. Brooke et al., eds., Church and Government in the Middle Ages: Essays Presented to C.R. Cheney on His 70th Birthday (Cambridge, England: Cambridge University Press, 1976), 77-91.
697. Campbell, James, "Some Twelfth-Century Views of the Anglo-Saxon Past," Peritia, 3(1984), 131-50.
698. Chibnall, Marjorie, "Charter and Chronicle: The Use of Archive Sources by Norman Historians," in C. Brooke et al., eds., Church and Government in the Middle Ages: Essays Presented to C.R. Cheney on His 70th Birthday (Cambridge, England: Cambridge University Press, 1976), 1-17.
699. Flint, Valerie I., "World History in the Early Twelfth Century: The Imago mundi of Honorius Augustodunensis," in R. Davis et al., eds., The Writing of History in the Middle Ages: Essays Presented to Richard William Southern (Oxford: Oxford University Press, 1981), 211-38.
700. ------, "The Historia regnum britanniae of Geoffrey Monmouth: Parody and Its Purpose. A Suggestion," Speculum, 54(1979), 447-68.
701. Gibson, Margaret, "History at Bec in the Twelfth Century," in R. Davis et al., eds., The Writing of History in the Middle Ages: Essays Presented to Richard William Southern (Oxford: Oxford University Press, 1981), 167-86.
702. Grandsen, Antonia, "Realistic Observation in Twelfth-Century England," Speculum, 47(1972), 29-51.
703. Guenée, Bernard, "Les prèmiers pas de l'histoire de l'historiographie en Occident au XIIe siècle," Académie des

inscriptions et belles lettres. Comptes rendus des séances, 1983, 136-52.
704. Hahn, Thomas, "The Medieval Oedipus," Comparative Literature, 32(1980), 225-37.
705. Leckie, Jr., William J., The Passage of Dominion: Geoffrey of Monmouth and the Periodization of Insular History in the Twelfth Century (Toronto: University of Toronto Press, 1981).
706. Legge, Mary D., "Anglo-Norman Hagiography and the Romances," Medievalia et humanistica, 6(1975), 41-49.
707. Liebeschütz, Hans, Medieval Humanism in the Life and Writings of John of Salisbury (London: Warburg Institute, University of London, 1950).
708. McKeon, Richard, "Poetry and Philosophy in the Twelfth Century: The Renaissance of Rhetoric," Modern Philology, 43(1945-46), 217-34.
709. Murphy, James J., "The Teaching of Latin as a Second Language in the 12th Century," Historiographica Linguistica, 7(1980), 159-75.
710. Sargent-Baur, Barbara N., "Dux bellorum, rex militum, roi fainéant: la transformation d'Arthur au XIIe siècle," Moyen Age, 90(1984), 357-73.
711. Southern, Richard W., "The Letters of Abelard and Heloise," Medieval Humanism and Other Studies (Oxford: B. Blackwell, 1970), 86-.
712. ------, "Aspects of the European Tradition of Historical Writing: 2. Hugh of St. Victor and the Idea of Historical Development," Transactions of the Royal Historical Society, 5th ser., 21(1971), 159-79.
713. ------, "Peter of Blois: A Twelfth Century Humanist?" Medieval Humanism and Other Studies (Oxford: B. Blackwell, 1970), 105-32.
714. Stock, Brian, "Medieval Literacy, Linguistic Theory, and Social Organization," New Literary History, 16(1984-85), 13-29.
715. Thomson, Rodney M., "William of Malmesbury as Historian and Man of Letters," Journal of Ecclesiastical History, 29(1978), 387-413.
716. Vitz, Evelyn Birge, "Type et individu dans l'autobiograhie médiévale: étude d'Historia calamitatum," Poétique, 6(1975): 426-45.

717. Ziolkowski, Jan, Alan of Lille's Grammar of Sex: The Meaning of Grammar to a Twelfth-Century Intellectual (Cambridge, MA: Medieval Academy of America, 1985).

4.4.2 Related Entries

Section 2.1.1: 47; section 2.2: 142; section 4.1: 480; section 4.2: 486, 495; section 4.3.l: 548; section 4.3.2: 581; section 4.3.4: 621; section 4.4.l: 659-662, 664, 665; section 4.4.3: 718, 720, 725, 742, 754; section 4.6: 826, 828.

4.4.3 Vernacular

718. Bautier, Robert H., ed., La France de Philippe Auguste; le temps de mutation: actes du Colloque international, Paris, 1980 (Paris: Centre national de la recherche scientifique, 1982).

Fifty papers presented to a 1980 conference include the section, "Les mutations intellectuelles: la langue et la littérature," with papers by P. Bourgain ("L'emploi de la langue vulgaire dans la littérature au temps de Philippe Auguste"), J. Monfrin ("L'emploi de la langue vulgaire dans les actes diplomatiques du temps de Philippe Auguste"), and A. Vernet ("La littérature latine au temps de Philippe Auguste").

719. Benton, John F., "The Court of Champagne as a Literary Center," Speculum, 36(1961), 551-91.

Explores "the relationship between life and imaginative writing" in the twelfth century by identifying and discussing several authors in four categories: regular court attendees, court authors, letter-writers, and those who wrote about the court. Concludes with general assessments of Henry the Liberal (1152-1181) and Countess Marie (1145-1198) as patrons, and compares Champagne with other literary centers.

720. Blacker-Knight, Jean, "From historia to estoire: Literary Form and Social Function of the Twelfth-Century Old French Verse

and Latin Prose Chronicle of the Anglo-Norman regnum." Ph.D. dissertation: University of California, Berkeley, 1984.

"This dissertation explores the political, social, and aesthetic needs of audiences of twelfth-century historical narratives and the structural qualities of the texts written to meet those needs. The primary materials used in this study include Latin prose histories by William of Malmesbury, Orderic Vitalis, and Geoffrey of Monmouth and Old French verse histories by Gaimar, Wace, and Benoit de Sainte-Maure." (Author's abstract)

721. Bloch, R. Howard, Medieval French Literature and Law (Berkeley: University of California Press, 1977).

Argues that contemporary French vernacular literature reflected the twelfth-century transition from combat to litigation for the resolution of conflict.

722. Boutet, Dominique, "Les chansons de geste et l'affermissement du pouvoir royal (1100-1250)," Annales: économies, sociétés, civilisations, 37(1982), 3-14.

One constant runs throughout the many and otherwise varied chansons de geste: Kingship is both valuable and powerful, with sentiments especially strong in the later years of the genre and after the reign of Philip Augustus (1165-1223).

723. Burgess, Glyn S., Marie de France: An Analytical Bibliography, Research Bibliographies & Checklists, 21 (London: Grant and Cutler, 1977); Marie de France: An Analytical Bibliography: Supplement, Research Bibliographies & Checklists, 21.2 (London: Grant and Cutler, 1986).

The 1977 bibliography contains 558 entries divided into the categories of manuscripts; editions, translations, and adaptations; books and articles; dissertations; and addenda. Citations are annotated and many include references to book reviews.

724. Cormier, Raymond J., "Tradition and Sources: The Jackson-Loomis Controversy Re-examined," Folklore, 83(1972), 101-21.

R. Loomis maintains that Celtic mythology serves as the principal source for the Arthurian tradition, and K. Jackson champions the position that the raw material of these myths has a far broader origin. Cormier compares the methodology, qualifications, transmission, parallels, and regard for folk traditions of these scholars, citing the leading works of these schools of thoughts.

725. Dronke, Peter, Medieval Latin and the Rise of European Love Lyric, 2d ed., 2 vols. (Oxford: Clarendon Press, 1968).
Explores the development of love poetry from the eleventh to the thirteenth centuries. Somewhat more attention is given to vernacular than to Latin verse. Volume one contains analysis and discussion; volume two consists of 150 texts, most of which are edited here for the first time.

726. Flori, J., "La notion de chevalerie dans la chansons de geste du XIIe siècle," Moyen Age, 81(1975), 211-44, 407-45.
A detailed vocabulary study that examines the conventions of literary chivalry and the literary function of the knight. Prior to 1180 the knight is depicted as a mounted, specially-equipped warrior. After this date he embodies the familiar ideals of the chivalrous knight, a transformation consistent with social changes discussed in item 111 in section 2.1.2.

727. Frappier, Jean, Chrétien de Troyes, l'homme et l'oeuvre (Paris: Hatier-Boivin, 1957). Translated by R. Cormier as Chretien de Troyes: The Man and His Work (Athens, OH: Ohio University Press, 1982).
The leading full-length study of Chrétien (c. 1135-1183). Chapters on Chrétien, his minor works, each of his major works, and his originality and influence. Includes a bibliography updated to 1978.

728. Freytag, Hartmut, Die Theorie der allegorischen Schriftdeutung und die Allegorie in deutschen Texten besonders des 11. und 12. Jahrhunderts (Bern: Francke Buchhandlung, 1982).
Ranges from discussion of allegorical theory based on contemporary Latin texts, to the application of this theory to vernacular German texts, to consideration of audience and reception (both hearing and reading). Copious notes and substantial bibliography.

729. Hanning, Robert W., The Individual in Twelfth-Century Romance (New Haven: Yale University Press, 1977).
For a period of about 30 years secular poetry, particularly courtly vernacular narratives, embraced notions of self-awareness acquired from Latin monastic works. The romances of Chrétien (c. 1135-1183) and several others represent the former; Peter Abelard's (1079-1142) autobiography and the life of Christina of Markyate (c. 1096-1160) embody the latter.

730. Kelly, Douglas, Chrétien de Troyes: An Analytic Bibliography (London: Grant and Cutler, 1976).
Over 120 pages of intermittent comments and citations to editions, works concerning problems of editing, bibliographies and critical reviews, and scholarly studies. Citations are unannotated.

731. Menard, Philippe, Les "lais" de Marie de France: contes d'amour et d'aventure du Moyen Age (Paris: Presses universitaires de France, 1979).
The best overall assessment of Marie de France's lais vis-à-vis the twelfth century. The leading English overview is E. Mickel, Marie de France (New York: Twayne Publishers, 1974).

732. Nykrog, Per, "The Rise of Literary Fiction," in R. Benson and G. Constable, eds., Renaissance and Renewal in the Twelfth Century (Cambridge, MA: Harvard University Press, 1982), 593-612.
Distinguishes between fictional literature and literary fiction, then accounts for the emergence of the latter in the 1160s and 1170s. (For example, the chansons de geste are fictional but not literary, whereas Chrétien's Erec possesses both attributes.) Includes a bibliographical note.

733. Pickford, Cedric E. and R. Last, eds., The Arthurian Bibliography, 2 vols. (Cambridge, England: D.S. Brewer, 1981-83).
Volume one contains an author arrangement of nearly 9,500 entries; volume two is a detailed subject index.

734. Raybin, David B., "The Development of a Leisured Class in Twelfth-Century Northern France and England: Mental Changes as Indicated Through the Patterned Examination of Literature and Society." Ph.D. dissertation: Columbia University, 1981.

Analyzes twelfth-century romances in the context of historical and literary patterns, and reconstructs a chronological pattern of the ideological development and mental structures of an emerging leisure class that underwrote the composition of these works.

735. Reiss, Edmund et al., Arthurian Legend and Literature: An Annotated Bibliography, 2 vols. (New York: Garland, 1984).

Volume one, devoted to the Arthurian legend and literature of the Middle Ages, contains 3,074 entries, most of which are lightly annotated. Twelve chapters arrange citations to scholarly works in such categories as reference, literary contexts, individual figures (Arthur, Lancelot, etc.), and non-Arthurian works using Arthurian elements. Subject and name indexes included.

736. Scholz, Manfred G., Hören und Lesen: Studien zur primären Rezeption der Literatur im 12. und 13. Jahrhundert (Wiesbaden: R. Steiner, 1980).

Studies the primary reception of twelfth- and thirteenth-century Middle High German texts. ("Primary reception" here means the mode of reception, either reading or hearing, by all recipients of the text, not just the principal or author's intended audience as conventionally meant by the phrase.) Concludes that the reading public for these texts was considerably larger than most scholars estimate. Includes an extensive bibliography.

737. Thurston-Taylor, Ruth E., "A Medieval Romance Model: Studies in French Fiction of the Twelfth and Thirteenth Centuries." Ph.D. dissertation: University of Oregon, 1982.

Presents a romance model consisting of seven necessary archetypes: "the individual adventure of certain elected knights, forest and water boundaries to the Other World, the conquering of supernatural figures, objects and worlds during the quest-adventure, fin'amor and all its conventions, a dream structure, a problematic world or universe, and an overall mythical structure."

738. Topsfield, L.T., Chrétien de Troyes: A Study of the Arthurian Romances (Cambridge, England: Cambridge University Press, 1981).
Though principally a work of synthesis and introduction, provides an overall view of Chrétien (c. 1135-1183) as a moral philosopher drawing on a sizable cultural inheritance of Celtic myth and contemporary and classical intellectual traditions.

739. ------, Troubadours and Love (Cambridge, England: Cambridge University Press, 1975).
Surveys the troubadors and the poetic evolution of their works from the early twelfth century, through the generations of 1170 and 1200, and well into the thirteenth century. Contains many biographical sketches. See section 2.2 for works on the social aspects of courtly love.

740. Tyson, Diana B., "Patronage of French Vernacular History Writers in the Twelfth and Thirteenth Centuries," Romania, 100:398(1979), 180-222.
Identifies and examines early vernacular history writers and their patrons. Concludes that patronage of vernacular French history was greater in England in the twelfth century before leadership shifted to the continent in the thirteenth. See related item 661 in section 4.4.1.

741. Ungureanu, Marie, La bourgeoisie naissante: société et littérature bourgeoises d'Arras aux XIIe et XIIIe siècles (Arras: Commission des monuments historiques du Pas-de-Calais, 1955).
Examines the social meaning of several genres of literature following a general introduction to bourgeois life in Arras during the twelfth and thirteenth centuries.

4.4.3 Additional Works

742. Archambault, Paul J., "Erec's Search for a New Language: Chrétien and Twelfth-Century Science," <u>Symposium</u>, 35(1981), 3-17.
743. Berkvam, Doris Desclais, <u>Enfance et maternité dans la littérature francais des XIIe et XIIIe siècles</u> (Paris: H. Champion, 1981).
744. Bezzola, Reto R., <u>Les origines et la formation de la littérature courtoise en Occident (500-1200)</u>, 3 vols. (Paris: H. Champion, 1944-63).
745. Bloch, R. Howard, <u>Etymologies and Genealogies: A Literary Anthropology of the French Middle Ages</u> (Chicago: University of Chicago Press, 1983).
746. Bouvier-Ajam, Maurice, "Chrétien de Troyes dans son temps," <u>Europe</u>, 60:642(1982), 16-26.
747. Bowden, Betsy, "The Art of Courtly Copulation," <u>Medievalia et humanistica</u>, 9(1979), 67-85.
748. Bruckner, Matilda T., <u>Narrative Invention in Twelfth-Century French Romance: The Convention of Hospitality, 1160-1200</u> (Lexington, KY: French Forum, 1980).
749. Doss-Quinby, Eglal, <u>Les refrains chez les trouvères du XIIe siècle au début du XIVe</u> (New York: P. Lang, 1984).
750. Gnädinger, Louise, <u>"Eremetica": Studien zur altfranzösischen Heiligenvita des 12. und 13. Jahrhunderts</u> (Tübingen: M. Niemeyer, 1972).
751. Gouttebroze, Jean G., "Henry II Plantagenet, patron des historiographes anglo-normands de langue d'oil," in <u>La littérature angevine médiévale: actes du Colloque du Samedi, 1980</u> (Paris: H. Champion, 1981), 91-105.
752. Grundmann, Herbert, "Die Frauen und die Literatur im Mittelalter," <u>Archiv für Kulturgeschichte</u>, 26(1936), 129-61.
753. Hanning, Robert W., "The Social Significance of Twelfth-Century Chivalric Romance," <u>Medievalia et humanistica</u>, 3(1972), 3-29.
754. Holmes, Urban T., <u>Chrétien de Troyes</u>, Twayne's World Authors Series, 94 (New York: Twayne Publishers, 1970).
755. Huchet, Jean C., "Nom de femme et écriture féminine au Moyen Age: les lais de Marie de France," <u>Poétique</u>, 48(1981), 407-30.

756. Hunt, Tony, "The Emergence of the Knight in France and England, 1000-1200," Forum for Modern Language Studies, 17(1981), 93-114.
757. Hurst, Peter W., "The Encyclopaedic Tradition, the Cosmological Epic, and the Validation of the Medieval Romance," Comparative Criticism, 1(1979), 53-71.
758. Keller, Hans, "La chanson de geste et son public," in J. De Caluwé, ed., Mélanges de philologie et de littératures romanes offerts à Jeanne Wathelet-Willem (Liège: Marche romane, 1978), 257-85.
759. Kellogg, Judith L., "Economic and Social Tensions Reflected in the Romance of Chrétien de Troyes," Romance Philology, 39(1985), 1-21.
760. Köhler, Erich, "Il sistema sociologico del romanzo francese medievale," Medioevo romanzo, 3(1976), 321-44.
761. Legge, Mary D., "La précocité de la littérature Anglo-Normande," Cahiers de civilisation médiévale, 8(1965), 327-49.
762. Legros, Huguette, "Le vocabulaire de l'amitié, son évolution sémantique au cours du XIIe siècle," Cahiers de civilisation médiévale, 23(1980), 131-39.
763. Loomis, Roger S., Studies in Medieval Literature: A Memorial Collection of Essays (New York: B. Franklin, 1970).
764. ------, Arthurian Tradition and Chrétien de Troyes (New York: Columbia University Press, 1949).
765. ------, The Grail: From Celtic Myth to Christian Symbol (New York: Columbia University Press, 1963).
766. ------, The Development of Arthurian Romance (London: Hutchinson, 1963).
767. Maddox, Donald, "Roman et manipulation au 12e siècle," Poétique, 66(1986), 179-90.
768. Marrou, Henri I., Les troubadours (Paris: Editions du Seuil, 1961).
769. Paterson, Linda, "Knights and the Concept of Knighthood in the Twelfth-Century Occitan Epic," Forum for Modern Language Studies, 17(1981), 115-30.
770. Pirot, Francois, Recherches sur les connaissances littéraires des troubadours occitans et catalans des XIIe et XIIIe siècles (Barcelona: Real academia de buenas letras, 1972).

771. Robreau, Yvonne, L'honneur et la honte: leur expression dans les romans en prose du Lancelot-Graal (XIIe-XIIIe siècles) (Geneva: Droz, 1981).
772. Tomchak, Laurie Scott, "Wace's Work: Patronage, Repetition and Translation in the Roman de Rou." Ph.D. dissertation: University of California, Irvine, 1984.

4.4.3 Related Entries

Section 1.1: 16; section 2.1.2: 111; section 2.2: 136, 144, 146, 155, 157, 159, 161, 163; section 3.1: 239; section 4.1: 480; section 4.2: 495; section 4.4.1: 659-662, 668, 671; section 4.4.2: 681, 704, 710; section 4.6: 824, 827, 832, 834, 840.

4.5 Art and Architecture

773. Bautier, Robert H., ed., La France de Philippe Auguste; le temps de mutation: actes du Colloque international, Paris, 1980 (Paris: Centre national de la recherche scientifique, 1982).
> Fifty papers presented to a 1980 conference include the section, "Les mutations artistiques," with papers by F. Denchler ("Y a-t-il un style Philippe Auguste?") and M. Huglo ("La musique religieuse au temps de Philippe Auguste").

774. Bloch, Herbert, "The New Fascination with Ancient Rome," in R. Benson and G. Constable, eds., Renaissance and Renewal in the Twelfth Century (Cambridge, MA: Harvard University Press, 1982), 615-36.
> Inventories the renewed fascination with ancient Roman remains, both material and literary, during the last third of the eleventh and throughout the twelfth centuries. A bibliographical note accompanies the work.

775. Boase, Thomas S., English Art, 1100-1216 (Oxford: Clarendon Press, 1953).
> Volume three of the Oxford History of English Art series provides both an overview for the uninitiated and scholarly

apparatus for the specialist. Bibliography is extensive but dated.

776. Bony, Jean, French Gothic Architecture of the 12th and 13th Centuries (Berkeley: University of California Press, 1983).
   At once a work of synthesis and interpretation, studying in depth both the technical and cognitive aspects of the French style. Includes background chapters, then three substantial chapters on the twelfth century, over 400 photographs and illustrations, and a bibliography of nearly 700 titles on all aspects and styles of Gothic architecture.

777. Fergusson, Peter J., Architecture of Solitude: Cistercian Abbeys in Twelfth-Century England (Princeton: Princeton University Press, 1984).
   A general survey that observes "a conscious withdrawal from existing traditions" and "a cautious return to contemporary movements" (p. 101). Includes 45-page catalog, sizable bibliography, and appendix on builders.

778. Gerson, Paula Lieber, ed., Abbot Suger and Saint-Denis: A Symposium (New York: Metropolitan Museum of Art, 1986).
   Collection of 22 well-illustrated papers from Metropolitan Museum of Art symposium. Essays grouped under "Monastic Life," "Political and Social History," "Architecture," "Library and Literature," "Sculpture and Mosaics," and "Stained Glass and Metalwork." Contributors include G. Constable, E. Bournazel, J. Bony, R. Hanning, and L. Grodecki.

779. Haussherr, Reiner, ed., Die Zeit der Staufer, 5 vols. (Stuttgart: Württembergisches Landesmuseum, 1977-79).
   The record of a 1977 Stuttgart exhibition. Includes the catalog (784 pages of descriptions alone); illustrations, reproductions, and maps; and two volumes of essays covering most aspects of Hohenstaufen civilization.

780. Horn, Walter, "Survival, Revival, Transformation: The Dialectic of Development in Architecture and Other Arts," in R. Benson and G. Constable, eds., Renaissance and Renewal in the

Twelfth Century (Cambridge, MA: Harvard University Press, 1982), 711-58.

The value of the twelfth-century revival of classical architecture was not the development of or a direct contribution to a true renaissance, rather the furtherance of a dialectic which culminated in the renaissance of the fifteenth and sixteenth centuries. In this dialectical model the medieval antithesis of the abstract and the figurative (the latter represented by periodic classical renascences, especially Romanesque and Gothic architecture and sculpture) created the conditions necessary for the higher revival and transformation of the Renaissance.

781. Kauffmann, Claus M., Romanesque Manuscripts, 1066-1190 (London: H. Miller, 1975).

Principally a catalog of British illuminated manuscripts from this period with an introduction that serves as a topical overview. Over 100 manuscripts described and over 350 illustrations included.

782. Kitzinger, Ernst, "The Arts as Aspects of a Renaissance," in R. Benson and G. Constable, eds., Renaissance and Renewal in the Twelfth Century (Cambridge, MA: Harvard University Press, 1982), 637-70.

"The Artistic Revival in Rome," "Methods and Motivations of the Roman Revival," and "Italy Outside of Rome" are discussed in this overview of the twelfth-century Italian classical revival. Concludes that these Italians largely expressed what E. Panofsky terms "surface classicism," whereas transalpine countries later developed an "intrinsic classicism."

783. ------, "Byzantine Contribution to Western Art of the Twelfth and Thirteenth Centuries," Dumbarton Oaks Papers, 20(1966), 25-47.

A summary statement presented to a 1965 symposium of the same title. (A synopsis of the meeting is contained in the volume.) Answers affirmatively the question about the influence of Byzantine art on Western art during the central Middle Ages, arguing that Byzantine ideals of the human form schooled Western artists until they were able to

make their own reconciliation with the classical past and
thereby develop an independent style in mature Gothic art.

784. Pächt, Otto, The Rise of Pictorial Narrative in Twelfth-
Century England (Oxford: Clarendon Press, 1962).
   Two chapters of this brief work remain particularly useful:
   "The Twelfth-Century Renaissance of the Classical Tradi-
   tion" and "Pictorial Representation and Liturgical Drama."

785. Panofsky, Erwin, Gothic Architecture and Scholasticism
(Latrobe, PA: Archabbey Press, 1951).
   Draws strong parallels between "the new style of thinking
   and the new style of building" from their inception in the
   mid-twelfth century through their flowering in the
   thirteenth.

786. Sauerländer, Willibald, "Architecture and the Figurative
Arts: The North," in R. Benson and G. Constable, eds., Renaissance and Renewal in the Twelfth Century (Cambridge, MA: Harvard
University Press, 1982), 671-710.
   Defines "renaissance" literally to mean a classical
   revival. Reviews twelfth-century architecture and
   figurative art for evidence of classical content, concluding that "twelfth-century renaissance" might be an
   accurate expression in a quantitative sense but not in
   terms of a self-conscious revival of classical forms.

787. Scher, Stephen K., The Renaissance of the Twelfth Century:
An Exhibition Organized by Stephen K. Scher (Providence: Museum
of Art, Rhode Island School of Design, 1969).
   A 220-page catalog for a 1969 exhibition by the same name.
   Includes extensive text, notes, several bibliographies, and
   essays by B. Lyon ("Was There a Renaissance of the Twelfth
   Century?"), W. Cahn ("The Artist as Outlaw and apparatchik:
   Freedom and Constraint in the Interpretation of Medieval
   Art"), and S. Scher ("The Rebirth of Sculpture in the
   Eleventh and Twelfth Centuries").

788. Simson, Otto G. von, "The Cistercian Contribution," in T.
Verdon, ed., Monasticism and the Arts (Syracuse: Syracuse
University Press, 1984), 115-37.

Gauges the contribution of Cistercian spirituality to twelfth-century and later medieval art and architecture. Bernard of Clairvaux's (1090-1153) concept of monastic life is embodied in Gothic sculpture generally and Cistercian architecture particularly.

789. Year 1200: A Symposium (New York: Metropolitan Museum of Art, 1975).
Twenty-seven symposium papers presented in conjunction with a 1970 exhibition at the Metropolitan Museum of Art. Includes some black-and-white reproductions, and papers by G. Ladner, C. Nordenfalk, P. Bloch, and others.

4.5 Additional Works

790. Branner, Robert, Chartres Cathedral (New York: Norton, 1969).
791. Courtenay, Lynn T., "Where Roof Meets Wall: Structural Innovations and Hammer-Beam Antecedants, 1150-1250," in P.O. Long, ed., Science and Technology in Medieval Society, Annals of the New York Academy of Sciences, 441 (New York: New York Academy of Sciences, 1985), 89-124.
792. Crosby, Sumner M., The Royal Abbey of Saint-Denis: From its Beginnings to the Death of Suger, 475-1151, ed. and completed by P. Blum (New Haven: Yale University Press, 1987).
793. ------ et al., The Royal Abbey of Saint-Denis in the Time of Abbot Suger (1122-1151) (New York: Metropolitan Museum of Art, 1981).
794. Dodwell, Charles R., The Canterbury School of Illumination, 1066-1200 (Cambridge, England: Cambridge University Press, 1954).
795. Duby, Georges, Adolescence de la chrétienté occidentale, 980-1140 (Geneva: A. Skira, 1967). Translated by S. Gilbert as The Making of the Christian West (Geneva: A. Skira, 1967).
796. ------, L'Europe des cathédrales, 1140-1280 (Geneva: A. Skira, 1966). Translated by S. Gilbert as Europe of the Cathedrals, 1140-1280 (Geneva: A. Skira, 1966).

797. Fergusson, Peter J., "The Builders of Cistercian Monasteries in Twelfth Century England," in M. Lillich, ed., Studies in Cistercian Art and Architecture, Cistercian Studies Series, 69 (Kalamazoo: Cistercian Publications, 1984), 14-29.
798. Folda, Jaroslav, ed., Crusader Art in the Twelfth Century (Oxford, England: B.A.R., 1982).
799. Frugoni, Chiara, "L'iconographie de la femme au cours des Xe-XIIe siècles," Cahiers de civilisation médiévale, 20(1977), 177-88.
800. Glass, Dorothy F., Italian Romanesque Sculpture: An Annotated Bibliography (Boston: G.K. Hall, 1983).
801. Goss, Vladimir P., "Western Architecture and the World of Islam in the Twelfth Century," in V.P. Goss, ed., The Meeting of Two Worlds: Cultural Exchange Between East and West During the Period of the Crusades, Studies in Medieval Culture, 21 (Kalamazoo: Medieval Institute Publications, Western Michigan University, 1986), 361-75.
802. Hearn, M., Romanesque Sculpture: The Revival of Monumental Stone Sculpture in the Eleventh and Twelfth Centuries (Ithaca: Cornell University Press, 1981).
803. Heimann, Adelheid, "The Master of Gargilesse: A French Sculptor of the First Half of the Twelfth Century," Journal of the Warburg and Courtauld Institutes, 42(1979), 47-64.
804. Hèliot, Pierre, "Les transformations de l'architecture française au temps de Philippe Auguste," Bulletin de la Commission départementale d'histoire et d'archéologie du Pas-du-Calais, 11:3(1984 for 1983), 363-81.
805. Henderson, George D., Chartres (Hammondsworth: Penguin, 1968).
806. James, John, The Contractors of Chartres, 2 vols. (Dooralong, Australia: Mandorla, 1979-1981).
807. Kahn, Deborah, "England in Europe: The Norman World of Art," History Today, 36:3(March 1986), 34-9.
808. Kitzinger, Ernst, "A Virgin's Face: Antiquarianism in Twelfth-Century Art," Art Bulletin, 62(1980), 6-19.
809. Morgan, Nigel J., Early Gothic Manuscripts (I), 1190-1250 (Oxford: Oxford University Press, 1982).
810. Nauratil, Karl Anthony, Jr., "Labor, Patronage, and Social Structure in the Making of Medieval Architecture: France

and England, 1000-1300." Ph.D. dissertation: University of Toronto, 1986.
811. Norton, Christopher and D. Perk, eds., Cistercian Art and Architecture in the British Isles (Cambridge, England: Cambridge University Press, 1986).
812. Panofsky, Erwin, Abbot Suger on the Abbey Church of St. Denis and its Art Treasures, 2d ed., (Princeton: Princeton University Press, 1979).
813. Sauerländer, Willibald, "Abwegige Gedanken über frühgotische Architektur und 'The Renaissance of the Twelfth Century,'" in Etudes d'art médiéval offertes à Louis Grodecki (Paris: Ophrys, 1981), 167-79.
814. ------, Gotische Skulptur in Frankreich, 1140-1270 (Munich: Hirmer, 1970). Translated by J. Sondheimer as Gothic Sculpture in France, 1140-1270 (London: Thames & Hudson, 1972).
815. Sedlmayr, Hans, "Die Wende der Kunst im 12. Jahrhundert," in Probleme des 12. Jahrhunderts, Vorträge und Forschungen, 12 (Stuttgart: J. Thorbecke, 1968), 425-40.
816. Simson, Otto von, The Gothic Cathedral: Origins of Gothic Architecture and the Medieval Concept of Order, 2d ed. (New York: Pantheon, 1962).
817. Stalley, R.A., Architecture and Sculpture in Ireland, 1150-1350 (New York: Barnes & Noble, 1972).
818. Vergnolle, Eliane, "L'art en Angleterre aux XIe et XIIe siècles," Revue de l'art, 67(1985), 85-96.
819. Zarnecki, George, English Romanesque Sculpture, 1066-1140 (London: A. Tiranti, 1951).
820. ------, Later English Romanesque Sculpture, 1140-1210 (London: A. Tiranti, 1953).

4.5 Related Entries

Section 1.1: 23, 40; section 4.2: 482; section 4.3.1: 548; section 4.4.1: 662; section 4.6: 833.

4.6 Performing Arts

821. Ashley, Kathleen M., "The Fleury 'Raising of Lazarus' and Twelfth-Century Currents of Thought," Comparative Drama, 15(1981), 139-58.

The model of a twelfth-century transition from epic to romance literature and from an "abuse of power" to a humanistic theory of redemption outlined in R. Southern's Making of the Middle Ages (item 27 in section 1.1) serves as the framework for an analysis of this play. The Fleury Lazarus evidences both of Southern's Weltanschauungen.

822. Bevington, David, "The Staging of Twelfth-Century Liturgical Drama in the Fleury Playbook," Comparative Drama, 18(1984), 97-117.

Applies a stage-oriented analysis of the ten-play Fleury Playbook. Concludes that a common staging tradition existed which made certain assumptions about stage space and the architectural interiors of churches.

823. Crawford, James M., "The Secular Latin Comedies of Twelfth Century France." Ph.D. dissertation: Indiana University, 1977.

Investigates 15 works often called elegiac comedies. Identifies and describes four genres, many pieces of which might have been performed or intended for performance.

824. Halbach, Kurt H., Walther von der Vogelweide, 3d ed. (Stuttgart: J.B. Metzlersche, 1973).

An exhaustive review of the Walther literature to the early 1960s that also serves as a cursory biography. Supplemented by George F. Jones, Walther von der Vogelweide, Twayne's World Authors Series, 46 (New York, 1968).

825. Hughes, Anselm, "Music in the Twelfth Century," Early Medieval Music up to 1300, New Oxford History of Music, 2 (London: Oxford University Press, 1955), 287-310.

Though dated, and a descriptive survey rather than an analytical assessment, this remains the single best introduction to twelfth-century music. Another general overview is W. Waite, The Rhythm of Twelfth-Century Polyphony: Its Theory and Practice (New Haven, 1954).

826. Wright, Craig, "Leoninus, Poet and Musician," Journal of the American Musicological Society, 39(1986), 1-35.

Biographical sketch of one of the twelfth century's most important and prolific composers. Preceded by a profile of a typical composer of twelfth-century polyphonic church music and followed by an assessment of the magister's legacy.

4.6 Additional Works

827. Adolf, Helen, "Walther von der Vogelweide and the Awakening of Personality," in F. Raven et al., eds., German Studies in Honor of Edward Henry Sehrt (Coral Gables: University of Miami Press, 1968), 1-13.
828. Bate, Keith, "Twelfth-Century Latin Comedies and the Theatre," in F. Cairns, ed., Papers of the Liverpool Latin Seminar: Second Volume, 1979 (Liverpool: F. Cairns, 1979), 249-62.
829. Braet, Herman et al., eds., The Theatre in the Middle Ages (Louvain: Louvain University Press, 1985).
830. Cattin, Giulio, Il Medioevo, 2 vols. (Turin: Edizioni di Torino, 1977). Translated by S. Botterill as Music of the Middle Ages, 2 vols. (Cambridge, England: Cambridge University Press, 1984).
831. Dahan, Gilbert, "Les lamentations dans le drame religieux (XIe-XIIIe siècles)," Trétaux, 3(1981), 1-18.
832. Gruber, Jörn, Die Dialektik des Trobar: Untersuchungen zur Struktur und Entwicklung des occitanischen und französischen Minnesangs des 12. Jahrhunderts (Tübingen: N. Niemeyer, 1983).
833. Kaden, C., "Gotische Musik: Baukunst und Polyphonie im Mittelalter," Musik und Gesellschaft, 36(1986), 514-22.
834. Page, Christopher, "Music and Chivalric Fiction in France, 1150-1300," Proceedings of the Royal Musical Association, 111(1986 for 1984-85), 1-27.
835. Sanders, Ernest H., "Consonance and Rhythm in the Organum of the 12th and 13th Centuries," Journal of the American Musicological Society, 33(1980), 264-86.
836. Tischler, Hans, "The Evolution of the Magnus liber organi," Musical Quarterly, 70(1984), 163-74.

837. Van Deusen, Nancy, "Origins of a Significant Medieval Genre: The Musical 'Trope' up to the Twelfth Century," Rhetorica, 3(1983), 245-67.
838. Waddell, Chrysogonus, The Twelfth-Century Cistercian Hymnal, 2 vols., Cistercian Liturgy Series, 1 (Trappist, KY: Gethsemani Abbey, 1984).
839. Wallace, Robin, "The Role of Music in Liturgical Drama: A Revaluation," Music and Letters, 65(1984), 219-28.
840. Wenzel, Horst, "Typus und Individualität: zur literarischen Selbstdeutung Walthers von der Vogelweide," Internationales Archiv für Sozialgeschichte der deutschen Literatur, 8(1983), 1-34.
841. Wickham, Glynne W., The Medieval Theatre, new ed. (Cambridge, England: Cambridge University Press, 1987).

4.6 Related Entries

Section 1.1: 33; section 4.5: 773

5.0 ECONOMIC LIFE AND THE PHYSICAL ENVIRONMENT

5.1 The Economy, Urbanization, and Population

842. Carus-Wilson, E.M., "The English Cloth Industry in the Late Twelfth and Early Thirteenth Centuries," Economic History Review, 14(1944), 32-50.

Describes the structure of the early English cloth industry which resided in the towns of East Anglia and exported fine cloth made with imported dyestuffs to Italy and Spain, rivaling the cloth of Flanders.

843. Duby, Georges, Guerriers et paysans, VII-XIIe siècle: premier essor de l'économie européen (Paris: Gallimard, 1973). Translated by H. Clark as The Early Growth of the European Economy: Warriors and Peasants from the Seventh to the Twelfth Century (Ithaca: Cornell University Press, 1974).

Traces the economic development of strongly conservative Western Europe, focusing on how social attitudes influenced economic relationships. Of central importance was the ability of the landed class to increase rents by directing the activities of the peasants.

844. Farmer, D.L., "Some Price Fluctuations in Angevin England," Economic History Review, 9(1956), 34-43.

Sheds light on the character of price changes for major foodstuffs, finding that price levels varied enormously from year to year and were two-to-three times higher by the end of the century.

845. Freedman, Paul H., "An Unsuccessful Attempt at Urban Organization in Twelfth-Century Catalonia," Speculum, 54(1979), 479-91.
The town of Vich provides an Iberian example of a rising urban elite which successfully gained recognition from the bishop, though it failed to create an independent communal government. Such urban solidarity parallels developments in Italy and the Low Countries.

846. Genicot, Léopold, "Sur les témoignages d'accroissement de la population en occident du XIe au XIIIe siècle," Cahiers d'histoire mondiale, 1(1953), 446-62.
Surveys the sources for research on demographic trends and considers their limitations. Various kinds of documentary material tell about demographic change and lead to the same conclusion, that population expanded steadily in most areas between the eleventh and thirteenth centuries.

847. Halpérin, Jean, "Les transformations économiques aux XIIe et XIIIe siècles," Revue d'histoire économique et sociale, 28(1950), 21-34.
Postulates a "true revolution" in the economic life of Europe characterized by a growth in population, the rise of commerce and towns, and the commutation of labor services. Marks the beginning of an outpouring of research on medieval economic history following World War II.

848. Harvey, P.D., "The English Inflation of 1180-1220," Past and Present, 61(November 1973), 3-30.
Describes the impact of severe price inflation and finds a cause in the high quantity of silver imported during the period. The strong inflationary movement that resulted makes these four decades similar to the great inflationary period of the sixteenth century, which likewise resulted from a strong influx of silver.

849. Lewis, Archibald R., "Patterns of Economic Development in Southern France, 1050-1271," Studies in Medieval and Renaissance History, 3(1980), 55-83.

The economic expansion that began around 1050 was characterized by northern European and Italian merchants and pilgrims using the Rhône Valley for communication, trade, and travel, with the nobility of the Midi supporting budding urbanization. After 1150, these factors led to a broad agrarian expansion and a more mature form of urbanization featuring fairs and town industry.

5.1 Additional Works

850. Abulafia, David, The Two Italies: Economic Relations Between the Norman Kingdom of Sicily and the Northern Communes (Cambridge, England: Cambridge University Press, 1977).
851. Bautier, Robert H., ed., La France de Philippe Auguste: le temps de mutation: actes du Colloque international, Paris, 1980 (Paris: Centre national de la recherche scientifique, 1982).
852. Bolton, John L., The Medieval English Economy, 1150-1500 (Totowa, NJ: Rowman & Littlefield, 1980).
853. Brooke, Christopher N., London, 800-1216: The Shaping of a City (Berkeley: University of California Press, 1975).
854. Cipolla, Carlo M., Before the Industrial Revolution: European Society and Economy, 1000-1700, 2d ed. (New York: Norton, 1980).
855. Fossier, Robert, "La démographie médiévale: problèmes de méthode (Xe-XIIIe siècles)," Annales de démographie historique, ?(1975), 143-65.
856. Gimpel, Jean, La révolution industrielle du Moyen Age (Paris: Seuil, 1975). Translated (uncredited) as The Medieval Machine: The Industrial Revolution of the Middle Ages (New York: Holt, Rinehart and Winston, 1976).
857. Hendy, M. F., "Byzantium, 1081-1204: An Economic Reappraisal," Transactions of the Royal Historical Society, 5th series, 20(1970), 31-52.
858. Lopez, Robert S., The Commercial Revolution of the Middle Ages, 950-1350 (Cambridge, England: Cambridge University Press, 1976).
859. Miller, Edward, "England in the Twelfth and Thirteenth Centuries: An Economic Contrast?" English Historical Review, 24(1971), 1-14.

860. Moore, Ellen Wedemeyer, The Fairs of Medieval England (Toronto: Pontifical Institute of Mediaeval Studies, 1985).
861. Musset, Lucien, "Peuplement en bourgage et bourgs ruraux en Normandie du Xe au XIIIe siècle," Cahiers de civilisation médiévale, 9(1966), 177-208.
862. Pirenne, Henri, Medieval Cities, lectures translated by F. Halsey (Princeton: Princeton University Press, 1925).
863. Postan, Michael M., "The Rise of a Money Economy," Economic History Review, 14(1944), 123-34.
864. Reynolds, Susan, An Introduction to the History of English Medieval Towns (Oxford: Clarendon Press, 1977).
865. Russell, Josiah C., "Aspects démographiques des débuts de la féodalité," Annales: économies, sociétés, civilisations, 20(1965), 1118-27.

5.1 Related Entries

Section 1.1: 7; section 2.1.1: 53, 82; section 3.2: 327; section 4.3.1: 539; section 4.4.3: 759; section 5.2: 868, 870, 881, 884.

5.2 Agrarian Studies and Estate Administration

866. Bennett, Henry S., Life on the English Manor: A Study of Peasant Conditions, 1150-1400 (Cambridge: Cambridge University Press, 1937).

One of the first works to depart from an emphasis on legal history and concentrate on social and economic conditions. Presents a homogeneous society in which local differences receive less attention than common themes. Recent studies have largely modified Bennet's views but this work remains a point of departure.

867. Donkin, R.A., "The Disposal of Cistercian Wool in England and Wales during the Twelfth and Thirteenth Centuries," Citeaux, 8(1957), 108-31, 181-202.

Discusses the transport of Cistercian wool within England and Wales, and its export to cloth-making centers in Flanders and Italy. Wool was a major commodity in the commerce of the twelfth and thirteenth centuries, and

Cistercian monastic establishments in England and Wales exported the majority of their clip.

868. Donkin, R.A., "Settlement and Depopulation on Cistercian Estates during the 12th and 13th Centuries, Especially in Yorkshire," Bulletin of the Institute of Historical Research, 33(November 1960), 141-57.

Within the context of expanding population in the twelfth and thirteenth centuries, documents the depopulation of Cistercian lands in Yorkshire through the abbot's evictions when additional plots of land came to the monasteries. Coersion and violence occasionally resulted.

869. Dubled, Henri, "Administration et exploitation des terres de la seigneurie rurale en Alsace aux XIe et XIIe siècle," Vierteljahrschrift für Sozial- und Wirtschaftsgeschichte, 47(1960), 433-73.

Examines how the landed nobility of Alsace exploited their lands as population growth dismembered the landed family, the arable expanded rapidly, and communal feelings increased.

870. Duby, Georges, "Economie domainale et économie monétaire: le budget de l'Abbaye de Cluny entre 1080 et 1155," Annales: économies, sociétés, civilisations, 7(1952), 155-71.

Discusses the economic support enjoyed by the monastery of Cluny, especially the shift from land to money and precious metals. Considers the budgetary crisis of the early twelfth century that forced adaptations and resulted in a lower standard of living.

871. ------, L'économie rurale et la vie des campagnes dans l'occident médiéval (France, Angleterre, Empire, IXe-XVe siècles) (Paris: Aubier, 1962). Translated by C. Postan as Rural Economy and Country Life in the Medieval West (Columbia: University of South Cariolina Press, 1968).

A major synthesis tracing the development of the rural economy from the ninth to the fifteenth century. Significant research on the major issues of medieval rural economy and society receive attention. Concludes that while several common threads run through these centuries, medieval rural society was highly compartmentalized. Prosperity and depression coexisted in close proximity, confirming the diversity of the Middle Ages.

872. Duby, Georges, "Problemes d'économie seigneuriale dans la France du XIIe siècle," in Probleme des 12. Jahrhunderts, Vorträge und Forschungen, 12 (Stuttgart: J. Thorbecke, 1968), 161-67.

Summarizes recent scholarship and finds twelfth-century France experienced a stabilization of seigneurial patrimonies, an expansion of commerce and the use of money, and a strong expansion of agriculture.

873. Graves, Coburn V., "The Economic Activities of the Cistercians in Medieval Engalnd, 1128-1307," Analecta sacri ordinis cisterciensis, 13(1957), 3-60.

With the Cistercian exordium parvum as a standard from which to measure, presents a survey of economic activities on English Cistercian estates, concluding that the pursuit of the spiritual ideal often was subverted by economic circumstances. This proved true in all areas, but especially in the production and marketing of wool.

874. Harvey, Sally P., "The Extent and Profitability of Demesne Agriculture in England in the Later Eleventh Century," in T. Ashton et al., eds., Social Relations and Ideas: Essays in Honour of R.H. Hilton (Cambridge, England: Cambridge University Press, 1983), 45-72.

Continues the century-long debate over the character of the manorial economy. Agrees with Postan, Lennard, and Miller that land was given over to rent payers with the subsequent contraction of established demesnes, but argues this was a positive response to the political and economic climate of the century that maximized resources for cultivation.

875. Herlihy, David, "The Agrarian Revolution in Southern France and Italy, 801-1150," Speculum, 33(1958), 23-41.

A "crisis" in the ninth and tenth centuries, characterized by depression and impoverishment, was followed by a period of expansion and growing prosperity in the eleventh and twelfth centuries. Reintegration of estates, redeployment of labor to newly assarted lands, increased travel, and growth of towns epitomized the latter period.

876. Higounet, Charles, "L'expansion de la vie rurale au XIIe et XIIIe siècle," Information historique, 11(1953), 17-22.

Surveys the major works published during 1946-52 on twelfth- and thirteenth-century rural life, a particularly fertile period in which scholarship, bottled up during World War II, blossomed.

877. Lennard, Reginald, Rural England, 1086-1135: A Study of Social and Agrarian Conditions (Oxford: Clarendon Press, 1959).

A general survey of rural conditions which portrays English rural society as both established (with manor and village settlement the typical pattern) and complex (with differences derived from wealth and status). Subsistence agriculture was the order of the day.

878. Miller, Edward, The Abbey and Bishopric of Ely: The Social History of an Ecclesiastical Estate from the Tenth Century to the Early Fourteenth Century (Cambridge, England: Cambridge University Press, 1951).

A technical survey of this prominent ecclesiastical estate, focusing on the exploitation of lands as revealed in the Doomsday Book and on the revolution in monastic estate administration at Ely in the time of Henry I.

879. ------, "La société rurale en Angleterre (Xe-XIIe siècles)," in Settimane di studio del centro italiano de studi sull'alto medioevo: agricoltura a mondo rurale in occidente nell'alto medioevo, 1965 (Spoleto: Sede del Centro italiana di studi sull'alto medioevo, 1966), 111-34.

The economic expansion of the eleventh and twelfth centuries induced a consolidation of the class of landed lords along with a rise in population, leading to an emphasis on the commercial marketing of products to maintain the position of the aristocracy.

880. Perroy, Edouard, <u>La terre et les paysans en France aux XIIe et XIIIe siècles</u> (Paris: Société d'édition d'enseignement superieur, 1973).

Discusses the prominent aspects of French rural economy and society, using texts to illustrate major traits and changes regarding land holding, standards of living, agricultural techniques, and the geography of rural life.

881. Postan, Michael M., "The <u>famulus</u>: The Estate Labourer in the XIIth and XIIIth Centuries," <u>Economic History Review</u>, supplement 2 (London, 1954).

Reverses an earlier opinion ("The Chronology of Labour Services," <u>Transactions of the Royal Historical Society</u>, 4th ser., 20[1937], 169-93), now finding that <u>famuli</u> (workmen retained for continuous service) were fairly common on twelfth-century English manors. Changing economic and demographic patterns caused the <u>famulus</u> to replace the serf and the slave, a trend that continued and broadened in the later Middle Ages.

882. ------, "Glastonbury Estates in the Twelfth Century," <u>Economic History Review</u>, 5(1952-53), 358-67.

Postan begins a twenty-year debate with an assessment of the twelfth-century reorganization of the lands of Glastonbury Abbey as a response to declines in revenues sparked by increases in direct exploitation of lands, rising rents, and reduced cultivation. R.V. Lennard ("The Glasbonbury Estates: A Rejoinder," <u>Economic History Review</u>, 28[1975], 517-23; introduced by B.F. Harvey and E. Stone) holds that changes on Glastonbury lands did not represent a trend of declining cultivation and rising rents. Rather, change occurred in farm leasing arrangements, the results of which were local and accidental. See also related articles by Postan, "Glastonbury Estates in the Twelfth Century: A Reply," <u>Economic History Review</u>, 9(1956-57), 106-18; and Lennard, "The Demesnes of Glastonbury Abbey in the Eleventh and Twelfth Centuries," <u>Economic History Review</u>, 8(1955-56), 355-63.

883. Roehl, Richard, "Plan and Reality in a Medieval Monastic Economy: The Cistercians," <u>Studies in Medieval and Renaissance History</u>, 9(1972), 83-113.

Discusses the economic implications of a Cistercian program that included a plan for participation in the mainstream of economic life. The plan met slight resistance within the order and led to changes in the requirements of monastic life.

884. Witt, Ronald G., "The Landlord and the Economic Revival of the Middle Ages in Northern Europe, 1000-1250," <u>American Historical Review</u>, 76(1971), 965-88.

Finds that the economic revival was led by a prospering nobility not threatened by the rising urban merchants. Questions basic assumptions traceable to H. Pirenne and M. Bloch, and calls for a new synthesis of scholarship on the period.

5.2 Additional Works

885. Berman, Constance H., <u>Medieval Agriculture, the Southern French Countryside, and the Early Cistercians: A Study of Forty-Three Monasteries</u>, Transactions of the American Philosophical Society, 76 (Philadelphia: American Philosophical Society, 1986).
886. Bloch, Marc, <u>Les caractères originaux de l'histoire rurale française</u>, 2 vols. (Paris: A. Colin, 1931). Translated by J. Sondheimer as <u>French Rural History: An Essay on Its Basic Characteristics</u> (Berkeley: University of California Press, 1966).
887. Dyer, Christopher, <u>Lords and Peasants in a Changing Society: The Estates of the Bishopric of Worcester, 680-1540</u> (Cambridge, England: Cambridge University Press, 1980).
888. Hallam, H.E., <u>Rural England, 1066-1348</u>, Fontana History of England (London: Fontana Paperbacks, 1981).
889. Harvey, Barbara F., <u>Westminster Abbey and its Estates in the Middle Ages</u> (Oxford: Clarendon Press, 1977).
890. Herlihy, David, "Church Property on the European Continent, 701-1200," <u>Speculum</u>, 36(1961), 81-105.
891. ------, "The History of the Rural Seigneury in Italy, 751-1200," <u>Agricultural History</u>, 33(1959), 58-71.

892. Hilton, Rodney H., "The Content and Sources of English Agrarian History Before 1500," <u>Agricultural History Review</u>, 3(1955), 3-19.
893. Jones, P.J., "An Italian Estate, 900-1200," <u>Economic History Review</u>, 7(1956-57), 18-32.
894. King, Edmund, <u>Peterborough Abbey, 1086-1310: A Study in the Land Market</u> (Cambridge, England: Cambridge University Press, 1973).
895. ------, "The Tenurial Crisis of the Early Twelfth Century," <u>Past and Present</u>, 65(November 1974), 110-17.
896. Mane, Perrine, <u>Calendriers et techniques agricoles: France-Italie, XIIe-XIIIe siècles</u> (Paris: Le Sycomore, 1983).
897. Miller, Edward and J. Hatcher, <u>Medieval England: Rural Society and Economic Change, 1086-1348</u> (London: Longman, 1978).
898. North, Douglas C. and R. Thomas, "The Rise and Fall of the Manorial System: A Theoretical Model," <u>Journal of Economic History</u>, 31(1971), 777-803.
899. Reed, Clyde G. and T. Anderson, "An Economic Explanation of English Agrarian Organization in the Twelfth and Thirteenth Centuries," <u>Economic History Review</u>, 26(1973), 134-37.

5.2 Related Entries

<u>Section 2.1.1</u>: 52, 53; <u>section 3.2</u>: 327; <u>section 3.3</u>: 378; <u>section 5.1</u>: 843, 844, 847, 852, 854, 859.

PERSON-AS-SUBJECT INDEX

Numbers Refer to Bibliography Entries

Abelard --> Peter Abelard
Adelard of Bath   623, 627,
   628, 635
Adrian IV (Nicholas
   Breakespear; pope)   316
Ailred of Rievaulx   538, 682
Alan of Lille   149, 598, 602,
   690, 691, 717
Alberic of Reims   657
Alexander III (pope)   247,
   253
Alexander of Hales   552
Alexius I (emperor, Byzantium)
   423
Andreas Capellanus   670, 684
Anselm of Canterbury   217,
   463, 474
Anselm of Havelberg   558, 673
Arnold of Brescia   195
Augustine of Hippo   680
Bacon, Roger   33
Baldric of Bourgueil   428
Becket, Thomas   213, 217,
   222, 230, 263, 269, 279,
   389, 551

Bernard of Clairvaux   11,
   178, 308, 460, 490, 495,
   501, 503, 513, 518, 519,
   523, 531, 534, 553, 571,
   599, 788
Bernard of St. Maure   720
Bernard Silvester   629, 691
Blunt, John   623
Burchard of Worms   141
Chrétien of Troyes   727, 729,
   730, 738, 742, 746, 754,
   764
Christina of Markyate   729
Clarembald of Arras   601
Conrad III (Holy Roman
   Emperor)   255
Desiderius (abbot, Monte-
   cassino)   488
Eleanor of Acquitaine   276,
   277, 284
Francis of Assisi   481
Frederick I (Barbarossa; Holy
   Roman Emperor)   243, 244,
   255, 301, 303
Frutolf of Bamberg   673

Gaimar 720
Geoffrey of Monmouth 696, 700, 705, 720
Gerald of Wales 539, 556, 567-569, 575, 680
Gerhoch of Reichersberg 673
Gervase of Canterbury 678
Gilbert of Poitier 586, 590, 597
Gilbert Foliot 285
Glanville, Ranulf de 411
Gratian 250, 376, 380
Gregory VII (pope) 255
Guerric of Igny 531
Guibert of Nogent 120, 141, 143, 428, 500, 507, 516, 565, 677, 680
Héloise 125, 509, 570, 711
Henry I (king, England) 45, 48, 290, 291, 292, 375, 377
Henry II (king, England) 213, 217, 233, 259, 260, 265, 283, 372, 399, 661, 667, 751
Henry of Huntingdon 685
Henry the Liberal 719
Hildebert of Lavardin 688
Hildegard of Bingen 123, 477, 675
Honorius Augustodunensis 559, 624, 699
Hubert Walter 218
Hugh of St. Cher 552
Hugh of St. Victor 562, 590, 673, 676, 692, 712
Hugoccio of Bologna 139
Innocent III (pope) 184, 255, 319
Jean of Hanville 691
Joachim of Fiore 609, 612, 613, 619, 620, 673

John (king, England) 295, 384, 399
John II (emperor, Byzantium) 423
John of La Rochelle 552
John of Salisbury 545, 682, 707
John of Worcester 695, 697
Lanfranc of Bec 270
Langton, Stephen 149, 389, 539
Leonin 826
Lothar III (Holy Roman Emperor) 255
Louis VII (king, France) 238
Manuel I (emperor, Byzantium) 423
Marie of France 719, 723, 755
Neckam, Alexander 145, 649
Norbert of Xanten 512
Odo of Soissons 586
Orderic Vitalis 486, 491, 673, 720
Otloh of St. Emmeram 680
Otto of Freising 673
Paschal II (pope) 257
Peter Abelard 119, 509, 534, 547, 548, 550, 553, 558, 560, 563, 570, 586, 589, 590, 607, 646, 675, 677, 680, 711, 716, 729
Peter Comestor 149
Peter Lombard 584, 590, 594
Peter of Blois 713
Peter of Bruys 179, 193
Peter the Chanter 386, 539, 552
Peter the Hermit 435
Peter the Venerable 374, 490, 519, 548, 683
Peter Waldo --> Waldo, Peter

Philip I (king, France) 58
Philip II (Augustus; king, France) 58, 234, 365, 366, 377, 722
Ralph of Diceto 678
Ranulf de Glanville -->
  Glanville, Ranulf de
Raoul of Paris 139
Ratherius of Verona 680
Raymond Berengar IV 324
Richard I (king, England) 258, 271, 272, 399
Richard of Devizes 685
Robert the Monk 428
Roger of Howden 678
Roger of Salisbury 377, 379
Roger of Worcester 219
Rupert of Deutz 673
Siegebert of Gembloux 673
Stephen of Blois 267, 268, 278
Suger of St. Denis 680, 778, 812

Theobald of Canterbury 289
Thierry of Chartres 608, 627, 628, 635
Thurston of York 286
Urban II (pope) 217, 420, 421
Urso of Calabria 623
Vacarius 655
Victor III (pope) 488
Wace 720, 772
Waldo, Peter 173, 184, 203, 207
Walther von der Vogelweide 824, 827, 840
William of Conches 627, 628, 635
William of Malmesbury 673, 697, 715, 720
William of Newburgh 685
William of Poitiers 683
William of St. Thierry 531, 579
William Rufus (king, England) 215

AUTHOR INDEX

Numbers Refer to Bibliography Entries

Abels, R.   105
Abulafia, D.   850
Adolf, H.   827
Aers, D.   684
Alexander, J.W.   212, 213, 655
Alphandéry, P.   432
Altschul, M.   214
Anderson, T.   899
Angold, M.   246
Appleby, J.T.   258, 259
Archambault, P.J.   742
Arnold, B.   42
Arnold, M.   404
Ashley, K.M.   821
Ashton, T.   140, 874
Atiya, A.S.   415, 416
Avi-Yonah, R.S.   621
Avril, J.   364
Bachrach, B.   226
Baker, D.   26, 124, 130, 132, 542
Baldwin, J.W.   365, 377, 386, 539, 555, 591, 639
Baldwin, M.W.   247
Banani, A.   3

Barber, R.W.   260
Barlow, F.   215, 261-263
Baron, R.   692
Barrow, G.W.   323
Barthélemy, D.   337
Bartlett, R.J.   433, 556
Batany, J.   50, 59
Bate, K.   828
Bautier, R.H.   234, 264, 366, 540, 718, 773, 851
Beales, D.   459
Beaujouan, G.   622
Beck, H.   255
Beddie, J.S.   541
Beech, G.T.   43
Beeler, J.   417
Bennet, H.S.   866
Benson, R.L.   1, 2, 8, 248, 353, 381, 382, 487, 543, 549, 583, 587, 611, 622, 639, 645, 659, 673, 683, 732, 780, 782, 786
Benton, J.F.   2, 3, 500, 719
Berger, D.   187
Berkhout, C.T.   167

Berkvam, D.D.   743
Berman, C.H.   125, 885
Berman, H.J.   367
Bertini, F.   693
Best, G.   459
Bethell, D.   467
Bevington, D.   822
Bezzola, R.R.   744
Bienvenu, J.M.   135
Bisson, T.N.   57, 324, 325, 368
Blacker-Knight, J.   720
Blake, E.O.   434, 435
Bliese, J.   694
Bligny, B.   34
Bloch, H.   774
Bloch, M.   44, 886
Bloch, P.   789
Bloch, R.H.   721, 745
Bloomfield, M.W.   609
Blum, P.   792
Boase, R.   136
Boase, T.S.   775
Boehm, L.   436
Bolton, B.M.   124, 168-170, 468
Bolton, J.L.   852
Bonenfant, P.   60
Bonnassie, P.   61
Bony, J.   776, 778
Bornstein, D.   155
Borst, A.   171
Bosl, K.   62, 387
Bouchard, C.B.   63, 106, 326
Bourgain, P.   718
Bournazel, E.   95, 369, 778
Boussard, J.   234, 265
Boutet, D.   722
Bouton, J. de la Croix   501
Bouvier-Ajam, M.   746
Bowden, B.   747
Braet, H.   829

Brand, C.M.   249
Brand, P.   165
Branner, R.   790
Bredero, A.H.   502, 503
Bresc, H.   57
Brett, M.   45, 695
Broich, U.   661
Brooke, C.N.   35, 72, 137, 138, 156, 188, 285, 372, 469, 482, 554, 696, 698, 853
Brooke, R.   138
Brown, E.A.   46, 50
Brown, P.   4
Brown, R.A.   473, 504
Bruckner, M.T.   748
Brundage, J.A.   418, 437, 438, 582
Brunet, A.   650
Bryer, A.   542
Bumke, J.   157
Burgess, G.S.   723
Buschinger, D.   59
Büttner, H.   255
Bynum, C.W.   5, 456, 470, 483, 672
Caenegem, R.C. van   370-372, 388
Cahen, C.   64, 419
Cahn, W.   787
Cairns, F.   828
Callahan, T.   216
Campbell, J.   373, 697
Campbell, R.   582
Cantor, N.F.   6, 217, 484
Carpentier, E.   65
Carus-Wilson, E.M.   842
Casey, K.   107
Cassady, R.F.   266
Cattin, G.   830
Cazel, F.A.   332
Chandler, V.   158

Chatillon, J.   11, 457, 485,
    540, 582, 610, 646
Chedeville, A.   338
Cheney, C.R.   218, 305, 389
Cheney, M.G.   219, 491
Chenu, M.D.   177, 576, 592,
    615
Cheyette, F.L.   111
Chibnall, M.   220, 486, 698
Chodorow, S.A.   250
Christiansen, E.   439
Cipolla, C.M.   854
Clagett, M.   7
Clanchy, M.T.   557, 658
Classen, P.   33, 152, 640,
    673
Clementi, D.   491
Cloes, H.   577
Cohen, J.   108
Cohn, N.   189
Connell, C.W.   125
Constable, G.   1, 2, 8, 47,
    248, 353, 374, 381, 382,
    458, 459, 471, 487, 491,
    505, 506, 543, 549, 583,
    587, 611, 622, 639, 645,
    659, 673, 683, 732, 774,
    778, 780, 782, 786
Comtamine, P.   440
Cormier, R.J.   724
Coulborn, R.   103
Coupe, M.D.   507
Courtenay, L.T.   791
Couvreur, G.   139
Cowdrey, H.E.   420, 441, 488
Crawford, J.M.   823
Cricco, P.   489
Crombie, A.C.   631
Cronne, H.A.   267
Crosby, E.U.   48
Crosby, S.M.   792, 793
Crouch, D.   339

Dahan, G.   831
Dales, R.C.   593, 623
D'Alverny, M.T.   543, 624,
    625
Davis, R.H.   268, 695, 699,
    701
Davy, M.M.   578
Debord, A.   49
De Caluwé, J.   758
Décarreaux, J.   340
Déchanet, J.M.   579
Deêr, J.   251
Delaruelle, E.   55, 442
Delhaye, P.   594, 641
DeMause, L.   120
Denchler, F.   773
Denomy, A.J.   159
De Pinto, B.   490
Despy, G.   60
D'Haenens, A.   508
Dillard, H.P.   109
Dobozy, M.   239
Dodwell, C.R.   794
Donkin, R.A.   867, 868
Dossat, Y.   190
Doss-Quinby, E.   749
Dotto, G.   595
Douglas, D.C.   221
Dronke, P.   509, 647, 659,
    674, 675, 725
Dubled, H.   66, 67, 869
Dubois, J.   510
Duby, G.   8, 50, 55, 68-70,
    110-112, 140, 141, 160,
    177, 327, 511, 795, 796,
    843, 870-872
Duggan, A.   36
Duggan, C.   269, 390, 391
Duhamel-Amado, C.   113
Dumézil, G.   50
Dunbabin, J.   235
Durand, R.   71

Duvernoy, J.   191, 192
Dyer, C.   887
Eberhard, W.   558
Ehlers, J.   33, 596, 676
Eisenstadt, S.N.   46
Elm, K.   512
Elswijk, H.C. van,   597
Emden, A.   652
Engels, O.   297
English, B.   341
Epstein, A.W.   39
Erdmann, C.   421
Estrada, J.A.   172
Evans, G.R.   472, 513, 580, 581, 598, 632
Evergates, T.   51
Faith, R.   165
Farmer, D.L.   844
Farmer, S.   126
Fawtier, R.   236
Fearns, J.   193
Ferguson, C.D.   677
Ferguson, W.K.   9
Fergusson, P.J.   777, 797
Ferrante, J.M.   664
Ferruolo, S.C.   10, 642
Fiétier, R.   350
Fischer, K.   33
Fleckenstein, J.   104, 152
Fletcher, R.   328
Flint, V.I.   127, 559, 616, 643, 699, 700
Flori, J.   142, 726
Folda, J.   798
Foreville, R.   11, 72, 222, 306, 491, 514, 582
Forey, A.J.   443-445
Fossier, R.   52, 194, 855
Foucault, M.   177
Frappell, L.   40
Frappier, J.   727
Freed, J.B.   73, 342

Freedman, P.H.   329, 845
Freytag, H.   728
Frugoni, A.   195
Frugoni, C.   799
Fuhrmann, H.   240
Galasso, G.   343
Gallais, P.   447
Gandillac, M. de   11
Geary, P.J.   446
Genicot, L.   37, 74, 196, 392, 846
Gersh, S.   583
Gerson, P.L.   778
Ghellinck, J. de   584
Gibson, M.T.   270, 655, 701
Gieysztor, A.   128
Gillingham, J.   223, 271, 272, 393
Gilson, E.H.   599
Gimpel, J.   856
Glass, D.F.   800
Gnädinger, L.   750
Gold, P.   114
Gonnet, J.   173
Goss, V.P.   801
Gouttebroze, J.G.   751
Grabois, A.   129, 447, 544
Gracia, J.   600
Grandsen, A.   702
Grane, L.   560
Graves, C.V.   873
Green, J.A.   375
Greenway, D.   491
Gregory, T.   625
Griffe, E.   197, 198
Grisward, J.   50
Grodecki, L.   778
Gross, C.   585
Gruber, J.   832
Grundmann, H.   174, 175, 177, 752
Grunebaum, G. von   7

Guenée, B.   703
Guillemain, B.   75, 234
Gurevich, A.J.   665
Guth, K.   143, 545
Gwynn, A.O.   12
Hahn, T.   704
Hajdu, R.   115
Halbach, K.H.   824
Hallam, E.M.   237
Hallam, H.E.   888
Hallier, A.   515
Halpérin, J.   847
Hamilton, B.   130, 394
Hanning, R.W.   729, 753, 778
Häring, N.M.   561, 601, 611
Harper-Bill, C.   144, 473
Harrison, E.   105
Harvey, B.F.   882, 889
Harvey, P.D.   848
Harvey, R.   144
Harvey, S.P.   395, 874
Haskins, C.H.   13, 633, 648
Hatcher, J.   897
Hausmann, F.   255
Haussherr, R.   779
Haverkamp, A.   298
Hearn, M.   802
Heer, F.   14, 15
Hehl, E.D.   376
Heimann, A.   803
Héliot, P.   804
Helle, K.   53
Hellmann, M.   76
Henderson, G.D.   805
Hendy, M.F.   857
Herbers, K.   199
Herkenrath, R.M.   396, 397
Herlihy, D.   77, 116, 176, 875, 890, 891
Higounet, C.   876
Hill, B.D.   492
Hilton, R.H.   892
Hödl, L.   586
Holdsworth, C.J.   448, 491
Hollister, C.W.   38, 78, 79, 224-227, 232, 273, 274, 344, 377, 398, 422
Holmes, U.T.   7, 16, 145, 754
Holt, J.C.   54, 275, 393
Holt, P.M.   449
Horn, W.   780
Hoyt, R.S.   102
Huchet, J.C.   755
Hughes, A.   825
Huglo, M.   773
Huling, R.W.   678
Hunt, N.   493
Hunt, R.W.   649
Hunt, T.   756
Hurst, P.W.   757
Hyams, P.R.   165, 378
Hyde, J.K.   345
Jackson, S.L.   562
Jaeger, C.S.   146
Jakobs, H.   252
Jalby, R.   200, 201
James, J.   806
Javelet, R.   11, 474, 602, 617
Jeauneau, E.   11
Johnson, F.   176
Jolliffe, J.E.   228
Jolivet, J.   553
Jones, G.F.   824
Jones, P.J.   893
Jordan, K.   241
Jordan, W.C.   374
Kaden, C.   833
Kahn, D.   807
Kammler, H.   80
Kanner, B.   107
Kantor, J.   516
Kantorowicz, E.H.   7, 307
Kauffmann, C.M.   781
Kazhdan, A.P.   39, 666

Kealey, E.J.   229, 379, 626
Keefe, T.K.   226, 399
Keen, M.   147
Keller, H.   758
Kellogg, J.L.   759
Kelly, A.   276
Kelly, D.   730
Kennan, E.   308
Kibler, W.W.   277
Kienast, W.   299
King, E.   278, 894, 895
Kitzinger, E.   782, 783, 808
Klibansky, R.   7
Kluxen, W.   33, 617
Knowles, D.   17, 230, 279, 517-519
Koch, G.   117, 242
Köhler, E.   760
Koziol, G.   330
Krautheimer, R.   346
Kroeschell, K.   400
Kumlien, K.   81
Kupper, J.L.   347, 400
Kuttner, S.G.   371, 380, 381, 386
Lackner, B.K.   520
Ladner, G.   1, 789
Lafont, R.   192
Lally, J.E.   667
Lane, F.C.   348
Lange, H.   634
Langmuir, G.   108
Last, R.   733
Lawrence, H.   521
Leckie, Jr., W.J.   705
Leclercq, J.   11, 148, 178, 460, 493-495, 522-524, 587, 618
Legge, M.D.   706, 761
Le Goff, J.   50, 82, 110, 177, 588
Legros, H.   762

Lehmann, P.J.   679, 680
Lejeune, R.   681
Lekai, L.J.   525, 526
Lemarignier, J.F.   83, 369
Lennard, R.   877, 882
Le Patourel, J.H.   84, 231, 232, 280, 281
Lerner, R.   619
Lewis, A.R.   349, 849
Leyser, H.   496
Leyser, K.J.   85, 282, 300
Liebeschütz, H.   682, 707
Lilie, R.J.   423
Lillich, M.   797
Little, L.K.   152, 461, 644
Lobrichon, G.   610
Locatelli, R.   350
Long, P.O.   628, 637, 791
Longère, J.   149, 527
Loomis, R.S.   763-766
Lopez, R.S.   858
Lottin, D.O.   603
Loud, G.A.   351
Lourdaux, W.   178
Loyn, H.R.   668
Lund, N.   112
Luscombe, D.E.   554, 563, 589
Lynch, J.H.   497
Lyon, B.D.   86, 787
MacKinnon, H.   604
Maddox, D.   767
Magdalino, P.   309
Makdisi, G.   506
Maleczek, W.   310
Mane, P.   896
Manselli, R.   179, 202, 243, 540
Manteuffel, T.   87
Marrou, H.I.   768
Martin, J.   683
Martini, M.   203
Mayer, H.E.   424, 425

Mayr-Harting, H.   227, 283,
    475, 476, 565
McCrillis, L.N.   118
McDonnell, E.W.   462
McGinn, B.J.   18, 463, 612
McGuire, B.P.   528
McKeon, R.   546, 625, 708
McLachlan, E.P.   564
McLaughlin, M.M.   119, 120,
    547
Meade, M.   284
Meisel, J.   352
Menard, P.   731
Meyendorff, J.   463
Mickel, E.J.   731
Milis, L.   529
Miller, E.   859, 878, 879,
    897
Miller, R.P.   161
Milsom, S.F.   402-404
Moi, T.   684
Mollat, M.   149, 166, 184
Moller, H.   150
Molnar, A.   173
Monfrin, J.   718
Moolenbroek, J.J. van   530
Moore, E.W.   860
Moore, J.C.   151
Moore, R.I.   50, 141, 178,
    180, 204, 227, 476, 565
Morey, A.   285
Morgan, N.J.   809
Morris, C.   19, 426, 464
Morrison, K.F.   311
Mundy, J.H.   162, 331, 353
Munz, P.   244
Murdoch, J.   546, 625
Murphy, J.J.   709
Murray, A.   20
Musset, L.   83, 354, 861
Nauratil, Jr., K.A.   810
Nelson, J.L.   181

Nelson, L.H.   355
Newman, B.   477
Newman, C.A.   88, 232
Newman, F.X.   163
Newman, W.M.   89, 90
Nicholl, D.   286
Niel, F.   205
Nielson, L.O.   590
Nitze, W.A.   21
Nordenfalk, C.   789
Nörr, K.W.   382
North, D.C.   898
North, S.   144
Norton, C.   811
Norwich, J.J.   356
Nykrog, P.   732
Opll, F.   245
Orme, N.   566
Otte, G.   33
Ourliac, P.   91, 92, 357
Outhwaite, R.B.   137
Pacaut, M.   238, 253, 301
Pächt, O.   784
Packard, S.R.   22
Page, C.   834
Painter, S.   121, 332
Palmer, R.C.   405
Panofsky, E.   23, 785, 812
Paravicini, W.   373
Paré, G.M.   650
Parisse, M.   56, 93
Partner, N.F.   685
Pastor de Togneri, R.   94
Paterson, L.   769
Payen, J.C.   651, 669
Penco, G.   605
Pennington, K.   47, 254
Pennington, M.B.   463, 531
Perk, D.   811
Perroy, E.   880
Petit-Dutaillis, C.   296
Pfaff, V.   312, 313

Pickford, C.E.   733
Pierce, I.   144
Pirenne, H.   862
Pirot, F.   770
Planitz, H.   302
Platelle, H.   164
Poly, J.P.   95, 358
Pontal, O.   287
Poole, A.L.   96
Post, G.   406
Postan, M.M.   863, 881, 882
Powicke, F.M.   288, 652
Prawer, J.   46, 450, 451
Prestwich, J.O.   97
Pycke, J.   478
Rabinowitz, L.I.   131
Racinet, P.   532
Radding, C.M.   24
Rashdall, H.   652
Rathbone, E.   407
Raven, F.   827
Ray, R.D.   686
Raybin, D.B.   734
Reed, C.G.   899
Reeves, M.   613
Reiss, E.   735
Renna, T.J.   533, 534
Reuter, T.   58
Reynolds, S.   359, 360, 864
Richard, J.   98, 99
Richardson, H.G.   122, 383
Riché, P.   535, 554, 610
Richter, M.   567, 568, 660
Riedmann, J.   243
Riley-Smith, J.   427, 428, 452
Riou, Y.   447
Roberts, B.F.   569
Robertson, Jr., D.W.   570
Robreau, Y.   771
Roehl, R.   883
Rosenwein, B.H.   536

Rossetti, G.   110
Rouse, M.   549
Rouse, R.H.   549
Rousset, P.   453, 479
Rowland, R.J.   361
Ruiz Domenec, J.E.   100
Runciman, S.   206, 256, 429
Russell, J.B.   167, 182
Russell, J.C.   865
Ryan, J.   371, 386
Saltman, A.   289
Sanders, E.H.   835
Sanford, E.   25
Santini, L.   207
Sargent-Baur, B.N.   710
Sass, S.L.   408
Sauerländer, W.   786, 813, 814
Sayles, G.   383
Scher, S.K.   787
Schirmer, W.F.   661
Schlight, J.   233, 314
Schlösser, F.   670
Schmale, F.J.   255, 315
Schmid, K.   104
Schmitt, J.C.   671
Schmugge, L.   362
Schneider, A.   537
Scholz, B.W.   123
Scholz, M.G.   736
Schramm, M.   33
Schultz, H.J.   210
Schüppert, H.   687
Searle, E.   165
Sedlmayr, H.   815
Servatius, C.   257
Setton, K.   429
Sheehan, M.M.   153
Shideler, J.   333
Siberry, E.   430, 454
Sigal, P.A.   166, 480
Sikes, J.G.   550

Simson, O.G. von   788, 816
Skyum-Nielsen, N.   112
Smail, R.C.   431
Smalley, B.   11, 26, 551, 552, 614
Smith, L.   36
Sommerfeldt, J.R.   571
Sommerville, R.   47
Southern, R.W.   27-29, 232, 290, 291, 316, 498, 606, 645, 653-655, 711-713
Spätling, L.G.   481
Spear, D.S.   292
Squire, A.   538
Stalley, R.A.   817
Steindorff, L.   317
Steinen, W. von den   572, 688
Stenton, D.M.   384
Stenton, F.M.   101
Stevens, M.   662
Stiefel, T.   627, 628, 635, 636
Stock, B.   30, 625, 629, 637, 714
Stollberg, G.   573
Stone, E.   882
Strait, P.   334
Strayer, J.R.   7, 102, 103
Sutherland, D.W.   409
Swaan, W.   482
Swan, E.   455
Sylla, E.   546, 625
Takayama, H.   410
Taylor, C.H.   541
Tellenbach, G.   55
Thomas, R.   898
Thompson, S.   132
Thomson, R.M.   31, 574, 689, 715
Thouzellier, C.   177, 183, 184
Thuillier, P.   638

Thurston-Taylor, R.E.   737
Tierney, B.   318
Tillman, H.   319
Tischler, H.   836
Tomchak, L.S.   772
Topsfield, L.T.   738, 739
Toubert, P.   208
Treadgold, W.   10
Tremblay, P.   650
Trout, J.M.   465, 690
Turner, R.V.   293, 385, 411, 412, 663
Tyson, D.B.   740
Ullmann, W.   32, 321
Ungureanu, M.   741
Urry, W.   335
Valerio, A.   133
Van Deusen, N.   837
Van Engen, J.   499
Van Hoecke, W.   154
Vaughn, S.N.   294
Verdon, T.   788
Verger, J.   540, 553
Vergnolle, E.   818
Verhelst, D.   178
Vernet, A.   718
Vinay, T.   210
Vinogradoff, P.   378
Violante, C.   104, 110, 177
Vitz, E.B.   716
Vryonis, S.   3
Waddell, C.   838
Wade, F.   607
Waite, W.   825
Wakefield, W.L.   185
Waley, D.P.   363
Wallace, R.   839
Walther, D.   186
Ward, B.   463, 466
Ward, J.O.   40
Warren, W.L.   12, 233, 295, 413

Weimar, P.   33
Welkenhuysen, A.   154
Wenzel, H.   840
Werner, E.   134, 152
Werner, K.F.   58, 255, 373
West, D.C.   620
West, F.J.   414
Wetherbee, W.   691
Wheeler, P.M.   656
White, Jr., L.   630
Wickham, G.W.   841
Widmer, B.   608
Wightman, W.E.   336
Wild, G.   211
Wilks, M.   554

Williams, A.   609
Williams, E.A.   575
Williams, J.R.   657
Wilpert, P.   607
Witt, R.G.   884
Wolf, G.   303
Wright, C.   826
Young, C.R.   41, 218
Zarnecki, G.   819, 820
Zielinski, H.   304
Zimdars-Swartz, S.   620
Zimmerman, A.   33, 561
Zinn, G.   463
Ziolkowski, J.   717